Betty Crocker®

Sunday Dinner

COOKBOOK

DESERET
BOOK

BICENTENNIAL
1807
WILEY
2007
BICENTENNIAL

Wiley Publishing, Inc.

ISBN-10: 1-59038-719-8
ISBN-13: 978-1-59038-719-1

Cataloging-in-Publication Data is available upon request from the Library of Congress.

Manufactured in China

10 9 8 7 6 5 4 3 2 1

General Mills

Publisher, Books and Magazines: Sheila Burke

Manager, Cookbook Publishing: Lois Tlusty

Recipe Development and Testing: Betty Crocker Kitchens

Photography and Food Styling: General Mills Photography Studios and Image Library

Wiley Publishing, Inc.

Publisher: Natalie Chapman

Executive Editor: Anne Ficklen

Editor: Kristi Hart

Production Director: Diana Cisek

Cover Design: Suzanne Sunwoo

Wiley Bicentennial Logo: Richard J. Pacifico

Interior Design and Layout: Elizabeth Brooks

Manufacturing Manager: Kevin Watt

The Betty Crocker Kitchens seal guarantees success in your kitchen. Every recipe has been tested in America's Most Trusted Kitchens™ to meet our high standards of reliability, easy preparation and great taste.

FIND MORE GREAT IDEAS AND SHOP
FOR NAME-BRAND HOUSEWARES AT
BettyCrocker.com

Dear Friends,

Do you remember Sunday dinners at Grandma's house, surrounded by aunts, uncles, cousins, and an abundance of good food? For many families, Sunday dinner is a time of gathering together. As warm, tantalizing smells emanate from the kitchen, it is a time to relax and reconnect with the people we love most dearly. It is a time for sharing old memories and creating new ones, a time for nourishing the spirit as well as the body.

Delicious meals shared with family and friends make memories that linger long after the last bite. Whether your Sunday tradition is a meat-and-potatoes dinner for twelve or a simple potluck gathering, *Betty Crocker Sunday Dinner Cookbook* has the recipes you need. You'll find tried-and-true classics such as Traditional Cornbread, Buttermilk Biscuits, Country Potato Salad, Golden Onion Soup, Garlic Smashed Potatoes, New England Pot Roast and Baked Barbeque Chicken. And who can resist dessert? Select the perfect finish to your meal from favorite recipes like Fudge Pudding Cake, Pumpkin Cheesecake, Lemon Meringue Pie or Caramel Turtle Bars.

Over the years, Betty Crocker has earned the reputation of being your best friend in the kitchen. Now—from her kitchen to yours—Betty Crocker shares mouthwatering recipes especially selected for your favorite meal of the week. With so many recipes to choose from, you're sure to find something your whole family will love!

Warmly,

Contents

Breads & Rolls

Herb Focaccia and Herb Glaze

6 FOCACCIA

The fresh herbs used in the glaze for this bread enlivens its wonderful, homey flavor. Make this traditional Italian bread the day before you plan on using it and warm before serving.

2 packages active dry yeast

1/4 teaspoon sugar

1 cup warm water

3 cups all-purpose flour

1/4 cup finely chopped onion

3 tablespoons vegetable oil

1 teaspoon salt

Herb Glaze (right)

1. Mix yeast, sugar and water in small bowl; let stand 5 minutes.

2. Blend remaining ingredients except Herb Glaze in large bowl; stir in yeast mixture to form a soft dough. Turn dough out onto floured surface. Knead dough 5 minutes until smooth and elastic. Place dough in greased bowl; cover and let rise in warm place 1 hour.

3. Grease baking sheet. Punch dough down; divide evenly into 6 pieces. Shape each piece into 5-inch circle; place on baking sheet. Cover; let rise 20 minutes.

4. Heat oven to 400°F. Brush top of each bread with Herb Glaze. Bake 15 to 18 minutes until light golden brown.

HERB GLAZE

1 tablespoon chopped fresh or 1/2 teaspoon dried thyme leaves

1 tablespoon chopped fresh or 1/2 teaspoon dried basil leaves

1 egg, beaten

Mix all ingredients.

1 SERVING: Calories 300 (Calories from Fat 70); Fat 8g (Saturated 1g); Cholesterol 35mg; Sodium 410mg; Carbohydrate 50g (Dietary Fiber 2g); Protein 9g

Pepper-Cheese Twists

18 TWISTS

Freshly ground black pepper adds a spicy kick to the twists. These are easy to make ahead; just cover them tightly with plastic wrap and refrigerate until ready to bake. They go great with clam chowder or tomato soup.

1/2 package (17 1/4 ounces) frozen puff pastry sheets, thawed

1 egg, beaten

1 cup shredded Cheddar cheese (4 ounces)

2 teaspoons black pepper

1. Heat oven to 425°F.

2. Roll sheet of dough into 18 x 12-inch rectangle; brush with beaten egg. Sprinkle cheese over half of rectangle; fold remaining half over cheese and press edges to seal.

3. Brush dough with egg; sprinkle with pepper. Cut pastry lengthwise into 1/2-inch strips. Twist strips and place on cookie sheet. Bake 10 to 12 minutes or until light golden brown.

1 SERVING: Calories 110 (Calories from Fat 70); Fat 8g (Saturated 3g); Cholesterol 35mg; Sodium 75mg; Carbohydrate 6g (Dietary Fiber 0g); Protein 3g

Easy Garlic-Cheese Biscuits

10 TO 12 BISCUITS

These melt-in-your-mouth biscuits are especially good with any meal. The next time you make them, experiment with a different cheese, such as smoky Cheddar or pizza mozzarella.

2 cups Original Bisquick® mix

2/3 cup milk

1/2 cup shredded Cheddar cheese (2 ounces)

1/4 cup margarine or butter, melted

1/4 teaspoon garlic powder

1. Heat oven to 450°F.

2. Mix Bisquick, milk and cheese to make a soft dough. Beat vigorously 30 seconds. Drop 10 to 12 spoonfuls dough onto ungreased cookie sheet.

3. Bake 8 to 10 minutes or until golden brown. Mix margarine and garlic powder; brush on warm biscuits before removing from cookie sheet. Serve warm.

1 BISCUIT: Calories 160 (Calories from Fat 90); Fat 10g (Saturated 3g); Cholesterol 10mg; Sodium 440mg; Carbohydrate 15g (Dietary Fiber 0g); Protein 3g

Pepperoni-Cheese Breadsticks

ABOUT 20 BREADSTICKS

Do a little dipping! Spaghetti sauce, pizza sauce and cheese sauce are all wonderful dips, especially when served warm.

2 3/4 cups Original Bisquick mix

1 cup shredded Monterey Jack cheese (4 ounces)

1 medium onion, finely chopped

1/2 cup sour cream

1/2 cup buttermilk

1 clove garlic, finely chopped

1 package (3 ounces) sliced pepperoni, chopped

1 cup grated Parmesan cheese

1. Heat oven to 375°F. Grease 2 cookie sheets. Stir all ingredients except Parmesan cheese until dough forms.

2. Drop dough by heaping tablespoonfuls into Parmesan cheese. Roll in cheese to coat. Roll into 8-inch breadsticks. Place about 1 1/2 inches apart on cookie sheets.

3. Bake 15 to 18 minutes or until golden brown.

1 BREADSTICK: Calories 150 (Calories from Fat 80); Fat 9g (Saturated 4g); Cholesterol 15mg; Sodium 450mg; Carbohydrate 11g (Dietary Fiber 0g); Protein 6g

Pepperoni-Cheese Breadsticks

Traditional Corn Bread

12 SERVINGS

Corn bread is one of America's favorite quick breads. Easy and quick to make, it's a hearty way to satisfy a longing for warm-from-the-oven homemade bread. Delicious when hot, corn bread is also wonderful when cooled, sliced and thickly spread with butter or jam, or when toasted the next day.

1 1/2 cups yellow cornmeal

1/2 cup all-purpose flour

1/4 cup shortening

1 1/2 cups buttermilk

2 teaspoons baking powder

1 teaspoon sugar

1 teaspoon salt

1/2 teaspoon baking soda

2 eggs

1. Heat oven to 450°F.

2. Grease round pan, 9 x 1 1/2 inches, or square pan, 8 x 8 x 2 inches. Mix all ingredients; beat vigorously 30 seconds.

3. Pour batter into pan. Bake until golden brown, 25 to 30 minutes Serve warm.

1 SERVING: Calories 140 (Calories from Fat 55); Fat 6g (Saturated 2g); Cholesterol 38mg; Sodium 370mg; Carbohydrate 19g (Dietary Fiber 1g); Protein 4g

Corn Bread Sticks

16 CORN BREAD STICKS

These hearty corn sticks are simply superb spread with honey-butter or drizzled with maple syrup. They also make dynamite dunkers dipped into a bowl of steaming chili.

1 cup Original Bisquick mix

1 cup yellow cornmeal

1 1/2 cups buttermilk

2 tablespoons vegetable oil

2 eggs

About 2 tablespoons yellow cornmeal

1. Heat oven to 450°F. Grease 2 loaf pans, 9 x 5 x 3 inches.

2. Stir Bisquick mix, 1 cup cornmeal, the buttermilk, oil and eggs until blended. Pour into pans. Sprinkle with 2 tablespoons cornmeal.

3. Bake about 15 minutes or until toothpick inserted in center comes out clean. Remove from pans. Cut each loaf crosswise into 8 sticks.

1 STICK: Calories 95 (Calories from Fat 35); Fat 4g (Saturated 1g); Cholesterol 30mg; Sodium 130mg; Carbohydrate 13g (Dietary Fiber 1g); Protein 3g

Corn Bread Sticks

Buttermilk Biscuits

ABOUT 10 BISCUITS

Buttermilk makes these biscuits tender and flavorful. The secret to fluffy biscuits is not overworking the dough. Once the shortening is cut into the flour, just a few quick stirs should make the dough form into a ball.

1/2 cup shortening

2 cups all-purpose flour

1 tablespoon sugar

2 teaspoons baking powder

1 teaspoon salt

1/4 teaspoon baking soda

About 3/4 cup buttermilk

1. Heat oven to 450°F.

2. Cut shortening into remaining ingredients except buttermilk in large bowl, using pastry blender or crisscrossing 2 knives, until mixture resembles fine crumbs. Stir in just enough buttermilk so dough leaves side of bowl and forms a ball.

3. Turn dough onto lightly floured surface. Knead lightly 10 times. Roll or pat 1/2 inch thick. Cut with floured 2 1/2-inch biscuit cutter. Place about 1 inch apart on ungreased cookie sheet.

4. Bake 10 to 12 minutes or until golden brown. Immediately remove from cookie sheet. Serve hot.

1 BISCUIT: Calories 200 (Calories from Fat 100); Fat 11g (Saturated 3g); Cholesterol 2mg; Sodium 390mg; Carbohydrate 22g (Dietary Fiber 0g); Protein 3g

Beaten Biscuits

24 BISCUITS

The beaten biscuit is a traditional Southern dish that dates back to the 1800s. Most biscuits are flaky and tender, but the beaten biscuit is hard and crisp. This texture is made when the dough is well beaten until it is smooth and elastic. Our suggestion of a wooden spoon or mallet works well for getting the texture just right.

1/4 cup shortening

2 cups all-purpose flour

2 teaspoons sugar

1/2 teaspoon salt

1/4 teaspoon baking powder

3/4 to 1 cup cold water

1. Heat oven to 400°F.

2. Cut shortening into flour, sugar, salt and baking powder with pastry blender in large bowl until mixture resembles coarse crumbs. Stir in 3/4 cup water; stir in additional water to make a stiff dough.

3. Turn dough onto lightly floured board. Beat dough with wooden spoon or mallet 5 minutes, turning and folding dough constantly. Roll or pat dough to 1/4-inch thickness. Cut with 2-inch biscuit cutter.

4. Place biscuits on ungreased cookie sheet; prick tops with fork. Bake 18 to 20 minutes or until golden brown.

1 BISCUIT: Calories 55 (Calories from Fat 20); Fat 2g (Saturated 1g); Cholesterol 0mg; Sodium 55mg; Carbohydrate 8g (Dietary Fiber 0g); Protein 1g

Popovers

6 POPOVERS

*Crusty on the outside and soft and moist on the inside, popovers are the perfect mate with roasts,
beef stew or any meal where there's a little juice to sop.*

1 cup all-purpose flour

1 cup milk

1/4 teaspoon salt

2 eggs

1. Heat oven to 450°F. Generously grease six 6-ounce custard cups.

2. Mix all ingredients with hand beater just until smooth (do not overbeat). Fill cups about half full. Bake 20 minutes.

3. Reduce oven temperature to 350°F. Bake 20 minutes longer. Immediately remove from cups. Serve hot.

1 POPOVER: Calories 120 (Calories from Fat 25); Fat 3g (Saturated 1g); Cholesterol 75mg; Sodium 140mg; Carbohydrate 18g (Dietary Fiber 0g); Protein 5g

Savory Quick Bread

6 SERVINGS

Using kitchen scissors makes the task of chopping dried tomatoes for this bread much easier.
Try cutting them before soaking in boiling water.

10 sun-dried tomato halves (not packed in oil)

2 cups Original Bisquick mix

1 package (8 ounces) feta cheese, coarsely crumbled

3/4 cup milk

3/4 cup roasted red bell (sweet) peppers (from
7-ounce jar), drained and finely chopped

1 tablespoon chopped fresh or 1 teaspoon dried
oregano leaves

1 tablespoon chopped fresh or 1 teaspoon dried
basil leaves

1 clove garlic, finely chopped

2 tablespoons olive or vegetable oil

1. Heat oven to 425°F. Grease square pan, 9 x 9 x 2 inches. Cover dried tomatoes with boiling water. Let stand 10 minutes; drain. Finely chop tomatoes.

2. Mix Bisquick, tomatoes, half of the cheese and the milk in medium bowl until dough forms. Mix remaining cheese, the bell peppers, oregano, basil, garlic and oil in small bowl. Drop half of the dough by tablespoonfuls closely together in irregular pattern in pan. Spoon half of the cheese mixture over dough. Drop remaining dough over cheese mixture. Top with remaining cheese mixture.

3. Bake about 20 minutes or until golden brown. Serve warm.

1 SERVING: Calories 325 (Calories from Fat 170); Fat 19g (Saturated 8g); Cholesterol 35mg; Sodium 1060mg; Carbohydrate 30g (Dietary Fiber 1g); Protein 10g

Savory Pull-Apart Bread

Skillet Cheddar Bread

6 SERVINGS

Save time by making your own baking mix. Start the bread by doing step 1 ahead.
Then, when you're ready, go on to the next steps and let it "bake."

2 cups all-purpose flour

1/4 cup nonfat dry milk

1 tablespoon sugar

1 teaspoon cream of tartar

1/2 teaspoon baking soda

1/2 teaspoon salt

1/4 cup firm butter or margarine

1/2 cup shredded Cheddar cheese (2 ounces)

3/4 cup water

1. Mix flour, dry milk, sugar, cream of tartar, baking soda and salt in resealable plastic food-storage bag.

2. Pour flour mixture into medium bowl. Cut in butter, using pastry blender or crisscrossing 2 knives, until mixture looks like cornmeal. Gently stir in cheese. Stir in water just until dough forms (do not overmix).

3. Grease 10-inch cast-iron skillet. Press dough into 3/4-inch-thick round. Cut into 6 wedges. Place wedges in skillet. Cover with aluminum foil. Cook over low heat about 10 minutes or until puffed and bottom is light brown. Turn wedges; cook about 10 minutes longer or until cooked through.

1 SERVING: Calories 270 (Calories from Fat 100); Fat 11g (Saturated 7g); Cholesterol 30mg; Sodium 320mg; Carbohydrate 36g (Dietary Fiber 1g); Protein 8g

Traditional White Bread

2 LOAVES, 16 SLICES EACH

Do you have a need to use less salt in your diet? If so, decrease sugar to 2 tablespoons and salt to 4 teaspoons. Substitute vegetable oil for the shortening. Each rising time will be 10 to 15 minutes shorter.

6 to 7 cups all-purpose or bread flour

3 tablespoons sugar

1 tablespoon salt

2 tablespoons shortening

2 packages active dry yeast

2 1/4 cups very warm water (120°F to 130°F)

Margarine or butter, melted

1. Mix 3 1/2 cups of the flour, the sugar, salt, shortening and yeast in large bowl. Add warm water. Beat with electric mixer on low speed 1 minute, scraping bowl frequently. Beat on medium speed 1 minute, scraping bowl frequently. Stir in enough remaining flour, 1 cup at a time, to make dough easy to handle.

2. Turn dough onto lightly floured surface. Knead about 10 minutes or until smooth and elastic. Place in greased bowl and turn greased side up. Cover and let rise in warm place 40 to 60 minutes or until double. Dough is ready if indentation remains when touched.

3. Grease bottoms and sides of 2 loaf pans, 8 1/2 x 4 1/2 x 2 1/2 or 9 x 5 x 3 inches, with shortening.

4. Punch down dough and divide in half. Flatten each half with hands or rolling pin into rectangle, 18 x 9 inches, on lightly floured surface. Roll dough up tightly, beginning at 9-inch side, to form a loaf. Press with thumbs to seal after each turn. Pinch edge of dough into roll to seal. Press each end with side of hand to seal. Fold ends under loaf. Place seam side down in pan. Brush loaves lightly with margarine. Cover and let rise in warm place 25 to 50 minutes or until double.

5. Move oven rack to low position so that tops of pans will be in center of oven. Heat oven to 425°F.

6. Bake 25 to 30 minutes or until loaves are deep golden brown and sound hollow when tapped. Remove from pans to wire rack. Brush loaves with margarine; cool.

1 SLICE: Calories 90 (Calories from Fat 10); Fat 1g (Saturated 0g); Cholesterol 0mg; Sodium 200mg; Carbohydrate 19g (Dietary Fiber 1g); Protein 2g

Pull-Apart Bread

1 LOAF, 12 SERVINGS

The delightful pull-apart loaf is also known as monkey bread or bubble loaf. For fun variations, after rolling the balls in butter, roll them in a cinnamon and sugar mixture or in a savory blend of fragrant herbs.

3 1/2 to 3 3/4 cups all-purpose flour

2 tablespoons sugar

1/2 teaspoon salt

1 package active dry yeast

1 cup milk

1/4 cup margarine or butter

1 egg

1/4 cup margarine or butter, melted

1. Grease 12-cup bundt cake pan or tube pan, 10 x 4 inches.

2. Mix 1 1/2 cups of the flour, the sugar, salt and yeast in 3-quart bowl. Heat milk and 1/4 cup margarine in 1-quart saucepan over medium-low heat, stirring frequently, until very warm (120°F to 130°F). Add milk mixture and egg to flour mixture. Beat on low speed until moistened; beat 3 minutes on medium speed. Stir in enough remaining flour to make dough easy to handle.

3. Turn dough onto lightly floured surface. Knead until smooth and elastic, about 5 minutes. Shape dough into 24 balls. Dip each ball of dough into the melted margarine. Layer evenly in pan. Cover and let rise in warm place until double, 20 to 30 minutes.

4. Heat oven to 350°F. Bake until golden brown, 25 to 30 minutes. Cool 2 minutes; invert onto heatproof serving plate. Serve warm.

1 SERVING: Calories 220 (Calories from Fat 80); Fat 9g (Saturated 2g); Cholesterol 20mg; Sodium 220mg; Carbohydrate 31g (Dietary Fiber 1g); Protein 5g

CHAPTER 2

Salads & Salad Dressings

Cranberry-Raspberry Salad

12 SERVINGS

The tang of the cranberry and the fruity coolness of the lemon gelatin make this salad a hit at any meal. We also think it will become a favorite of yours on the Thanksgiving table.

2 containers (12 ounces each) frozen cranberry- orange sauce

1 container (12 ounces) cranberry-raspberry sauce

1 package (6 ounces) lemon gelatin

2 cups boiling water

1. Lightly oil 6 1/2-cup ring mold.

2. Mix cranberry sauces together in large bowl. Dissolve gelatin in boiling water; stir into cranberry sauces. Pour into mold. Cover and refrigerate overnight.

3. Unmold salad. Garnish with watercress and cranberries if desired.

1 SERVING: Calories 190 (Calories from Fat 0); Fat 0g (Saturated 0g); Cholesterol 0mg; Sodium 60mg; Carbohydrate 49g (Dietary Fiber 2g); Protein 1g

Key Lime Fruit Salad

8 SERVINGS

For a quicker preparation, use a 20-ounce can of pineapple chunks, drained. For a similar tangy taste, use lemon instead of Key lime pie–flavored yogurt.

1 container (6 ounces) Key lime pie yogurt

2 tablespoons orange juice

2 cups fresh pineapple chunks

1 cup strawberry halves

2 cups green grapes

1 cup blueberries

2 cups cubed cantaloupe

1/4 cup flaked or shredded coconut, toasted*

1. Mix yogurt and orange juice.

2. Layer fruit in order listed in 2 1/2-quart clear glass bowl. Pour yogurt mixture over fruit. Sprinkle with coconut. Serve immediately.

*To toast coconut, bake coconut uncovered in ungreased shallow pan in 350°F oven 5 to 7 minutes, stirring occasionally, until golden brown.

1 SERVING: Calories 120 (Calories from Fat 20); Fat 2g (Saturated 1g); Cholesterol 0mg; Sodium 25mg; Carbohydrate 25g (Dietary Fiber 2g); Protein 2g

Key Lime Fruit Salad

24-Hour Fruit Salad and Whipped Cream Dressing

8 SERVINGS

Whipped Cream Dressing (right)

1 can (16 1/2 ounces) pitted light or dark sweet cherries, drained

2 cans (20 ounces each) pineapple chunks in juice, drained and 2 tablespoons juice reserved for dressing

3 oranges, cut into small chunks*

1 cup miniature marshmallows

1. Make Whipped Cream Dressing.

2. Gently toss dressing and remaining ingredients in large glass or plastic bowl. Cover and refrigerate at least 12 hours to blend flavors but no longer than 24 hours. Store remaining salad covered in refrigerator.

*2 cans (11 ounces each) mandarin orange segments, drained, can be substituted for the oranges.

WHIPPED CREAM DRESSING

2 large eggs, beaten

2 tablespoons sugar

2 tablespoons white vinegar or lemon juice

2 tablespoons reserved pineapple juice

1 tablespoon butter or margarine

Dash of salt

3/4 cup whipping (heavy) cream

1. Heat all ingredients except whipping cream just to boiling in 1-quart saucepan over medium heat, stirring constantly; cool.

2. Beat whipping cream in chilled medium bowl with electric mixer on high speed until stiff.

3. Fold in egg mixture.

1 SERVING (about 1 cup): Calories 255 (Calories from Fat 90); Fat 10g (Saturated 6g); Cholesterol 80mg; Sodium 35mg; Carbohydrate 40g (Dietary Fiber 3g); Protein 4g

Mandarin Salad and Sweet-Sour Dressing

6 SERVINGS

Enjoy one of our most requested salads, especially by men. The nutty almonds and the sweet mandarin slices blend perfectly together in this salad. Even better, add some grilled chicken pieces or cooked shrimp.

1/4 cup sliced almonds

1 tablespoon plus 1 teaspoon sugar

Sweet-Sour Dressing (below)

1/2 small head lettuce, torn into bite-size
pieces (3 cups)

1/2 bunch romaine, torn into bite-size
pieces (3 cups)

2 medium stalks celery, chopped (1 cup)

2 medium green onions, thinly sliced (2 tablespoons)

1 can (11 ounces) mandarin orange segments, drained

1. Cook almonds and sugar in 1-quart saucepan over low heat, stirring constantly, until sugar is melted and almonds are coated; cool and break apart.

2. Make Sweet-Sour Dressing.

3. Toss almonds, dressing and remaining ingredients.

SWEET-SOUR DRESSING

1/4 cup vegetable oil

2 tablespoons sugar

2 tablespoons white or cider vinegar

1 tablespoon chopped fresh parsley

1/2 teaspoon salt

Dash of pepper

Dash of red pepper sauce

Shake all ingredients in tightly covered container. Refrigerate until serving.

1 SERVING (about 1 1/3 cups): Calories 180 (Calories from Fat 110); Fat 12g (Saturated 2g); Cholesterol 0mg; Sodium 220mg; Carbohydrate 18g (Dietary Fiber 2g); Protein 2g

Mandarin Salad and Sweet-Sour Dressing

Antipasto Salad and Vinaigrette

Have fun choosing different sausages, cheese, olives and peppers for this salad. Look for different varieties at a neighborhood Italian market, specialty store or deli.

1/4 cup Italian olives

8 ounces fresh mozzarella cheese, drained and cubed

4 ounces sliced Italian salami

4 ounces sliced Italian capicolla, prosciutto or fully cooked smoked Virginia ham

4 ounces marinated Italian peppers

1 jar (8 ounces) marinated mushrooms, drained

1/4 cup chopped fresh basil leaves

Vinaigrette (below)

Arrange all ingredients except basil on 6 salad plates. Sprinkle with fresh basil. Serve with Vinaigrette.

VINAIGRETTE

1/3 cup olive oil

3 tablespoons red wine vinegar

1 clove garlic, crushed

Mix all ingredients.

1 SERVING: Calories 345 (Calories from Fat 245); Fat 27g (Saturated 9g); Cholesterol 45mg; Sodium 1080mg; Carbohydrate 6g (Dietary Fiber 1g); Protein 20g

Italian New Potato Salad

8 SERVINGS

It's easy to tell when the potatoes are done: you should be able to just pierce them with a fork.

3/4 pound green beans

10 to 12 new potatoes (1 1/2 pounds), cut into fourths

1/4 cup water

1/2 cup Italian dressing or balsamic vinaigrette

1/4 cup chopped red onion

1 can (2 1/4 ounces) sliced ripe olives, drained

1. Cut beans in half if desired. Place beans, potatoes and water in 2-quart microwavable casserole. Cover and microwave on High 10 to 12 minutes, rotating dish 1/2 turn every 4 minutes, until potatoes are tender; drain.

2. Place beans and potatoes in large glass or plastic bowl. Pour dressing over vegetables; toss. Add onion and olives; toss.

1 SERVING: Calories 125 (Calories from Fat 65); Fat 7g (Saturated 1g); Cholesterol 0mg; Sodium 210mg; Carbohydrate 17g (Dietary Fiber 3g); Protein 2g

Italian New Potato Salad

Heartland Three-Bean Salad

12 SERVINGS

Three-bean salads are favorites in the heartland. But not everyone agrees on which three beans to include in this hearty salad. You can count on finding green beans and wax beans in most recipes. While many recipes—including ours—use kidney beans, there are some that call for lima beans instead. Of course, you can add lima beans to this recipe and enjoy a four-bean salad!

1 can (16 ounces) cut green beans, drained

1 can (16 ounces) cut wax beans, drained

1 can (15 ounces) kidney beans, drained

1 cup thinly sliced onion rings, cut in half

1 small bell pepper, finely chopped (about 1/2 cup)

2 tablespoons chopped fresh parsley

2/3 cup vinegar

1/2 cup sugar

1/3 cup vegetable oil

1/2 teaspoon pepper

1/2 teaspoon salt

2 slices bacon, crisply cooked and crumbled

1. Mix beans, onion, bell pepper and parsley in 3-quart bowl.

2. Mix remaining ingredients in 1 1/2-quart saucepan. Heat vinegar mixture to boiling, stirring occasionally. Pour over beans; stir.

3. Cover and refrigerate, stirring occasionally, at least 3 hours or until chilled. Just before serving, sprinkle with bacon.

1 SERVING: Calories 160 (Calories from Fat 65); Fat 7g (Saturated 1g); Cholesterol 0mg; Sodium 400mg; Carbohydrate 23g (Dietary Fiber 4g); Protein 5g

Heartland Three-Bean Salad and Country Potato Salad (page 31)

Country Potato Salad and Cooked Salad Dressing

10 SERVINGS

Marinating the potatoes in the Italian dressing beforehand makes this a flavorful potato salad and one of the most requested favorites. Instead of the Cooked Salad Dressing, 1 cup of mayonnaise or salad dressing can be mixed in. (See photo on page 30.)

6 medium potatoes (about 2 pounds)

1/4 cup Italian dressing

Cooked Salad Dressing (right) or 1 cup
  mayonnaise

2 medium stalks celery, sliced (about 1 cup)

1 medium cucumber, chopped (about 1 cup)

1 large onion, chopped (about 3/4 cup)

6 radishes, thinly sliced (about 1/2 cup)

4 hard-cooked eggs, chopped

1. Heat 1 inch water (salted if desired) to boiling. Add potatoes. Cover and heat to boiling; reduce heat. Cook until tender, 30 to 35 minutes. Drain and cool slightly.

2. Peel potatoes; cut into cubes (about 6 cups). Toss warm potatoes with Italian dressing in 4-quart glass or plastic bowl. Cover and refrigerate at least 4 hours. Prepare Cooked Salad Dressing.

3. Add celery, cucumber, onion, radishes and eggs to potatoes. Pour Cooked Salad Dressing over top; toss. Refrigerate until chilled. Immediately refrigerate any remaining salad.

COOKED SALAD DRESSING

2 tablespoons all-purpose flour

1 tablespoon sugar

1 teaspoon ground mustard

3/4 teaspoon salt

1/4 teaspoon pepper

1 egg yolk, slightly beaten

3/4 cup milk

2 tablespoons vinegar

1 tablespoon margarine or butter

Mix flour, sugar, mustard, salt and pepper in 1-quart saucepan. Mix egg yolk and milk in small bowl; slowly stir into flour mixture. Cook over medium heat, stirring constantly, until mixture thickens and boils. Boil and stir 1 minute; remove from heat. Stir in vinegar and margarine. Place plastic wrap directly on surface; refrigerate until cool, at least 1 hour.

1 SERVING: Calories 290 (Calories from Fat 200); Fat 22g (Saturated 4g); Cholesterol 100mg; Sodium 210mg; Carbohydrate 20g (Dietary Fiber 2g); Protein 5g

Classic Creamy Potato Salad

10 SERVINGS

For a summery flavor and a cool crunch, we stir in 1/2 cup each thinly sliced radishes, chopped cucumber and chopped bell pepper.

6 medium boiling potatoes (2 pounds)

1 1/2 cups mayonnaise or salad dressing

1 tablespoon vinegar

1 tablespoon ground mustard

1 teaspoon salt

1/4 teaspoon pepper

2 medium stalks celery, chopped (about 1 cup)

1 medium onion, chopped (about 1/2 cup)

4 hard-cooked eggs, chopped

1. Heat 1 inch water (salted, if desired) to boiling. Add potatoes. Cover and heat to boiling; reduce heat to low. Boil gently 30 to 35 minutes or until potatoes are tender; cool slightly. Cut into cubes (about 6 cups).

2. Mix mayonnaise, vinegar, mustard, salt and pepper in large glass or plastic bowl. Add potatoes, celery and onion; toss. Stir in eggs. Cover and refrigerate at least 4 hours. Cover and refrigerate any remaining salad.

1 SERVING: Calories 350 (Calories from Fat 250); Fat 28g (Saturated 5g); Cholesterol 105mg; Sodium 480mg; Carbohydrate 21g (Dietary Fiber 2g); Protein 5g

Cold Cucumber Salad

12 SERVINGS

When the temperature is too hot to handle, try whipping up this cool salad. Even better, you can make it a day ahead of time.

1/2 cup sugar

1/3 cup water

1 teaspoon white pepper

1/2 teaspoon salt

1 1/2 cups cider vinegar

4 large cucumbers, peeled and thinly sliced

1/4 cup chopped fresh parsley

1. Mix sugar, water, white pepper and salt in medium saucepan. Heat mixture over medium-high heat to boiling and boil until sugar is dissolved; remove from heat and cool. Stir in vinegar.

2. Pour mixture over cucumber slices; sprinkle with parsley. Cover and refrigerate until ready to serve.

1 SERVING: Calories 50 (Calories from Fat 0); Fat 0g (Saturated 0g); Cholesterol 0mg; Sodium 100mg; Carbohydrate 13g (Dietary Fiber 1g); Protein 1g

Old-Fashioned Coleslaw

8 SERVINGS

Coleslaw is not an American invention. It is thought to have been brought to this country by either German or Dutch immigrants. The Dutch called their salad koolsla (cabbage salad). Our recipe blends sweet-and-tangy flavor with the richness of sour cream. If you prefer, you can leave out the carrot and bell pepper and toss in a chopped tart apple and 1/4 cup crumbled blue cheese for an apple-cheese slaw.

3 tablespoons sugar

2 tablespoons all-purpose flour

1 teaspoon ground mustard

1/2 teaspoon salt

1/8 teaspoon ground red pepper (cayenne)

1 egg

3/4 cup water

1/4 cup lemon juice

1 tablespoon margarine or butter

1/4 cup sour cream

1 pound green cabbage, shredded or finely chopped
    (about 6 cups)

1 medium carrot, shredded (about 1 cup)

1 small bell pepper, finely chopped (about 1/2 cup)

1. Mix sugar, flour, mustard, salt and red pepper in heavy 1-quart saucepan; beat in egg. Stir in water and lemon juice gradually until well blended. Cook over low heat 13 to 15 minutes, stirring constantly, until thick and smooth; remove from heat.

2. Stir in margarine until melted. Place plastic wrap directly on surface of dressing; refrigerate about 2 hours or until cool. Stir in sour cream.

3. Mix dressing, cabbage, carrot and bell pepper; toss well. Refrigerate at least 1 hour but no longer than 24 hours.

1 SERVING: Calories 85 (Calories from Fat 35); Fat 4g (Saturated 1g); Cholesterol 30mg; Sodium 190mg; Carbohydrate 12g (Dietary Fiber 2g); Protein 2g

Seven-Layer Salad

6 SERVINGS

This salad is a little mix of everything: crunchy, sweet, smoky and tangy. For less fat and fewer calories but still great flavor, use turkey bacon and low-fat or non-fat salad dressing.

6 cups bite-size pieces mixed salad greens

2 medium stalks celery, thinly sliced (1 cup)

1 cup thinly sliced radishes

1/2 cup sliced green onions (5 medium)

12 slices bacon, crisply cooked and crumbled

1 package (9 ounces) frozen green peas, thawed

1 1/2 cups mayonnaise or salad dressing

1/2 cup grated Parmesan cheese or shredded Cheddar cheese (2 ounces)

1. Place salad greens in large glass bowl. Layer celery, radishes, onions, bacon and peas on salad greens.

2. Spread mayonnaise over peas, covering top completely and sealing to edge of bowl. Sprinkle with cheese. Cover and refrigerate at least 2 hours to blend flavors but no longer than 12 hours. Toss before serving if desired. Cover and refrigerate any remaining salad.

1 SERVING: Calories 550 (Calories from Fat 480); Fat 53g (Saturated 10g); Cholesterol 50mg; Sodium 720mg; Carbohydrate 11g (Dietary Fiber 3g); Protein 10g

Greek Salad and Lemon Dressing

8 SERVINGS

Tangy feta cheese is Greek in origin and is traditionally made from sheep or goat milk. It is sometimes referred to as "pickled" cheese because it's cured and stored in its own salty whey brine.

Lemon Dressing (below)

7 ounces spinach, torn into bite-size pieces (5 cups)

1 head Boston lettuce, torn into bite-size

    pieces (4 cups)

1/2 cup crumbled feta cheese (2 ounces)

4 medium green onions, sliced (1/4 cup)

24 pitted ripe olives

3 medium tomatoes, cut into wedges

1 medium cucumber, sliced

1. Make Lemon Dressing.

2. Toss dressing and remaining ingredients.

LEMON DRESSING

1/4 cup vegetable oil

2 tablespoons lemon juice

1/2 teaspoon sugar

1 1/2 teaspoons Dijon mustard

1/4 teaspoon salt

1/8 teaspoon pepper

Shake all ingredients in tightly covered container.

1 SERVING (about 1 3/4 cups): Calories 120 (Calories from Fat 90); Fat 10g (Saturated 3g); Cholesterol 10mg; Sodium 320mg; Carbohydrate 6g (Dietary Fiber 2g); Protein 3g

Spinach-Shrimp Salad with Hot Bacon Dressing

4 SERVINGS

Buy fresh uncooked shrimp to cook yourself, or purchase freshly cooked shrimp. Frozen shrimp can save even more time because it is available already peeled and cooked, and it needs only to be thawed before tossing in the salad.

4 slices bacon, cut into 1-inch pieces

1/4 cup white vinegar

1 tablespoon sugar

1/4 teaspoon ground mustard

4 cups lightly packed bite-size pieces spinach leaves

1 cup sliced mushrooms (3 ounces)

1 cup crumbled feta cheese (4 ounces)

1/2 pound cooked, peeled, deveined medium

    shrimp

1. Cook bacon in 10-inch skillet over medium-high heat, stirring occasionally, until crisp. Stir in vinegar, sugar and mustard; continue stirring until sugar is dissolved.

2. Toss spinach, mushrooms, cheese and shrimp in large bowl. Drizzle hot bacon dressing over spinach mixture; toss. Serve immediately.

1 SERVING: Calories 200 (Calories from Fat 110); Fat 12g (Saturated 7g); Cholesterol 150mg; Sodium 670mg; Carbohydrate 7g (Dietary Fiber 1g); Protein 20g

Snappy Seafood Salad

4 SERVINGS

It's a snap to put this summer seafood salad together. Dress it up and add a nice texture and flavor with tender, young salad greens that you can purchase pre-mixed in place of the lettuce.

2 cups uncooked medium pasta shells (5 ounces)

2/3 cup mayonnaise or salad dressing

1 tablespoon chili sauce or cocktail sauce

1/3 cup small pitted ripe olives

3 cups bite-size pieces lettuce

1 package (8 ounces) frozen seafood chunks (imitation crabmeat), thawed

1 small tomato, cut into 8 wedges

1. Cook and drain pasta as directed on package. Rinse with cold water; drain.

2. Mix mayonnaise and chili sauce in large bowl. Add pasta and olives; toss. Add lettuce and seafood; toss. Serve with tomato wedges.

1 SERVING: Calories 480 (Calories from Fat 290); Fat 32g (Saturated 5g); Cholesterol 40mg; Sodium 870mg; Carbohydrate 36g (Dietary Fiber 2g); Protein 14g

Snappy Seafood Salad

Greek Pasta Salad

5 SERVINGS

Feta cheese is bursting with sharp, tangy, salty flavor. This crumbly cheese is traditionally made from goat's or sheep's milk, but due to its popularity is often made with cow's milk. Crumbled blue cheese, in place of the feta, is also good on this salad.

1 1/4 cups uncooked orzo or rosamarina pasta (8 ounces)

2 cups thinly sliced cucumber (about 2 small)

1 medium red onion, chopped (1/2 cup)

1/2 cup Italian dressing

1 medium tomato, chopped (3/4 cup)

1 can (15 ounces) garbanzo beans, rinsed and drained

1 can (2 1/4 ounces) sliced ripe olives, drained

1/2 cup crumbled feta cheese (2 ounces)

1. Cook pasta as directed on package; drain. Rinse with cold water; drain.

2. Mix pasta and remaining ingredients except cheese in large glass or plastic bowl. Cover and refrigerate at least 1 hour to blend flavors but no longer than 24 hours.

3. To serve, top salad with cheese.

1 SERVING: Calories 445 (Calories from Fat 155); Fat 17g (Saturated 3g); Cholesterol 15mg; Sodium 580mg; Carbohydrate 66g (Dietary Fiber 9g); Protein 16%

Caesar Salad

6 SERVINGS

1 clove garlic, cut in half

8 anchovy fillets, cut up*

1/3 cup olive or vegetable oil

3 tablespoons lemon juice

1 teaspoon Worcestershire sauce

1/4 teaspoon salt

1/4 teaspoon ground mustard

Freshly ground pepper

1 large or 2 small bunches romaine, torn into bite-size pieces (10 cups)

1 cup garlic-flavored croutons

1/3 cup grated Parmesan cheese

1. Rub large wooden salad bowl with cut clove of garlic. Allow a few small pieces of garlic to remain in bowl if desired.

2. Mix anchovies, oil, lemon juice, Worcestershire sauce, salt, mustard and pepper in salad bowl.

3. Add romaine; toss until coated. Sprinkle with croutons and cheese; toss.

*2 teaspoons anchovy paste can be substituted for the anchovy fillets.

1 SERVING (about 1 3/4 cups): Calories 165 (Calories from Fat 125); Fat 14g (Saturated 3g); Cholesterol 10mg; Sodium 430mg; Carbohydrate 6g (Dietary Fiber 1g); Protein 5g

Chicken Caesar Salad: Broil or grill 6 boneless, skinless chicken breast halves; slice diagonally and arrange on salads. Serve chicken warm or chilled.

Waldorf Salad

4 SERVINGS

Instead of apples, why not try fresh pears instead? Stirring in 2 tablespoons dried blueberries, cherries, cranberries or raisins is perfect for adding a tasty flavor and pretty color.

1/2 cup mayonnaise or salad dressing

1 tablespoon lemon juice

1 tablespoon milk

2 medium unpeeled red eating apples, coarsely chopped (2 cups)

2 medium stalks celery, chopped (1 cup)

1/3 cup coarsely chopped nuts

Salad greens, if desired

1. Mix mayonnaise, lemon juice and milk in medium bowl.

2. Stir in apples, celery and nuts. Serve on salad greens. Store remaining salad covered in refrigerator.

1 SERVING (about 3/4 cup): Calories 305 (Calories from Fat 250); Fat 28g (Saturated 4g); Cholesterol 15mg; Sodium 180mg; Carbohydrate 14g (Dietary Fiber 3g); Protein 2g

Waldorf Salad

CHAPTER 3

Soups & Stews

Chicken Tortellini Soup

8 SERVINGS

Cheese-stuffed tender pastas floating in steamy chicken broth will provide comfort and warmth to rejuvenate your soul. Some hot, homemade buttery biscuits might help, too.

1/4 cup margarine or butter

1/2 cup finely chopped onion

1/2 cup finely chopped celery

4 boneless skinless chicken breasts (about
    1 1/2 pounds), cut into 1-inch pieces

1/4 cup all-purpose flour

1/2 teaspoon pepper

4 1/2 cups chicken broth

1 package (16 ounces) cheese-filled tortellini, cooked

Parmesan cheese

1. Heat margarine in large saucepan until melted. Cook and stir onion, celery and chicken in margarine over medium heat about 8 minutes or until chicken is done.

2. Stir in flour and pepper; gradually add chicken broth. Cook over medium heat, stirring constantly, until mixture boils; boil 1 minute.

3. Stir in tortellini; heat until warm. Serve with Parmesan cheese.

1 SERVING: Calories 245 (Calories from Fat 110); Fat 12g (Saturated 3g); Cholesterol 85mg; Sodium 720mg; Carbohydrate 14g (Dietary Fiber 1g); Protein 21g

Vegetable–Cheddar Cheese Soup

8 SERVINGS

This creamy, colorful cheese soup is popular with adults and kids alike. Warm whole-grain bread or rolls are perfect for sopping up and dunking in the soup.

1/2 cup margarine or butter

1 cup carrot, finely chopped

1/2 cup onion, finely chopped

1/2 cup celery, finely chopped

2 medium zucchini, cut into 2-inch strips

1/2 cup all-purpose flour

1 teaspoon ground mustard

2 cups chicken broth

2 cups half-and-half

3 cups shredded Cheddar cheese (12 ounces)

1. Heat margarine in Dutch oven until melted. Cook carrot, onion and celery in margarine until softened. Stir in zucchini and cook about 2 minutes or until crisp-tender. Mix flour and mustard; stir into vegetable mixture.

2. Gradually stir in chicken broth and half-and-half. Cook over medium heat, stirring constantly until mixture boils; boil 1 minute. Slowly stir in cheese until melted.

1 SERVING: Calories 400 (Calories from Fat 295); Fat 33g (Saturated 15g); Cholesterol 65mg; Sodium 710mg; Carbohydrate 13g (Dietary Fiber 2g); Protein 15g

Golden Onion Soup

6 SERVINGS

Just pop this soup in the oven and come back in a couple hours; the soup bakes in the oven to a rich, golden goodness all on its own. It doesn't get any easier than that.

Parmesan Croutons (right)

1/4 cup margarine or butter

1 tablespoon packed brown sugar

1 teaspoon Worcestershire sauce

4 large onions (3/4 to 1 pound each), cut into
    fourths and sliced

2 cans (10 1/2 ounces each) condensed beef broth

2 soup cans water

1. Prepare Parmesan Croutons; reserve.

2. Reduce oven temperature to 325°F.

3. Heat margarine in 4-quart ovenproof Dutch oven until melted; stir in brown sugar and Worcestershire sauce. Toss onions in margarine mixture.

4. Bake uncovered, stirring every hour, until onions are deep golden brown, about 2 1/2 hours. Stir in broth and water; heat to boiling over high heat. Serve with Parmesan Croutons.

PARMESAN CROUTONS

1/4 cup margarine or butter

3 slices bread, cut into 1-inch cubes

Grated Parmesan cheese

Heat oven to 400°F. Heat margarine in rectangular pan, 13 x 9 x 2 inches, in oven until melted. Toss bread cubes in margarine until evenly coated. Sprinkle with cheese. Bake uncovered, stirring occasionally, until golden brown and crisp, 10 to 15 minutes.

1 SERVING: Calories 235 (Calories from Fat 155); Fat 17g (Saturated 4g); Cholesterol 5mg; Sodium 820mg; Carbohydrate 17g (Dietary Fiber 2g); Protein 5g

Golden Onion Soup

Chunky Tomato Soup

8 SERVINGS

A quick whirl in a blender or food processor will smooth out this soup without sacrificing any flavor.
Kids will love it if you stir in some cooked alphabet noodles.

2 tablespoons olive or vegetable oil

2 cloves garlic, chopped

2 medium stalks celery, coarsely chopped (1 cup)

2 medium carrots, coarsely chopped (1 cup)

2 cans (28 ounces each) whole Italian-style
    tomatoes, undrained

2 cups water

1 teaspoon dried basil leaves

1/2 teaspoon pepper

2 cans (14 1/2 ounces each) chicken broth

8 slices hard-crusted Italian or French bread, each
    1 inch thick, toasted

Grated Parmesan cheese, if desired

1. Heat oil in Dutch oven over medium-high heat. Cook garlic, celery and carrots in oil 5 to 7 minutes, stirring frequently, until carrots are crisp-tender.

2. Stir in tomatoes, breaking up tomatoes coarsely. Stir in remaining ingredients except toast and cheese. Heat to boiling; reduce heat. Cover and simmer 1 hour, stirring occasionally.

3. Place 1 slice toast in each of 8 bowls. Ladle soup over toast. Sprinkle with cheese. Serve immediately.

1 SERVING: Calories 175 (Calories from Fat 55); Fat 6g (Saturated 1g); Cholesterol 0mg; Sodium 840mg; Carbohydrate 26g (Dietary Fiber 3g); Protein 7g

Chicken Noodle Soup

4 SERVINGS

What's better than a warm, soothing bowl of golden chicken noodle soup? Even better, this soup can be made in under 30 minutes!

2 tablespoons olive or vegetable oil

2 cloves garlic, finely chopped

2 medium green onions, chopped (2 tablespoons)

1 medium carrot, sliced (1/2 cup)

2 cups cubed cooked chicken

1 cup 2-inch pieces uncooked spaghetti or 4 ounces uncooked egg noodles

1 tablespoon chopped fresh parsley or 1 teaspoon dried parsley flakes

1/2 teaspoon ground nutmeg

1/4 teaspoon pepper

1 bay leaf

3 cans (14 1/2 ounces each) chicken broth

1. Heat oil in 3-quart saucepan over medium heat. Cook garlic, onions and carrot in oil about 4 minutes, stirring occasionally, until carrot is crisp-tender.

2. Stir in remaining ingredients. Heat to boiling; reduce heat. Cover and simmer about 15 minutes, stirring occasionally, until spaghetti is tender.

3. Remove bay leaf.

1 SERVING: Calories: 360 (Calories from Fat 125); Fat 14g (Saturated 3g); Cholesterol 55mg; Sodium 1120mg; Carbohydrate 30g (Dietary Fiber 2g); Protein 31g

Chicken Noodle Soup

Vegetable-Beef Soup

Want to make this soup in a snap? Use 4 cups canned beef broth and 3 cups cut-up cooked beef for the Beef and Broth. You can also keep it speedy by using 1 cup each frozen corn kernels, peas and green beans for the fresh.

Beef and Broth (below)

1 ear corn

2 medium potatoes, cubed (2 cups)

2 medium tomatoes, chopped (1 1/2 cups)

1 medium carrot, thinly sliced (1/2 cup)

1 medium stalk celery, sliced (1/2 cup)

1 cup 1-inch pieces green beans

1 cup shelled green peas

1/4 teaspoon pepper

1. Prepare Beef and Broth. Add enough water to broth to measure 5 cups. Return strained beef and broth to Dutch oven.

2. Cut kernels from corn. Stir corn and remaining ingredients into broth. Heat to boiling; reduce heat to low. Cover and simmer about 30 minutes or until vegetables are tender.

BEEF AND BROTH

2 pounds beef shank cross-cuts or soup bones

6 cups cold water

1 teaspoon salt

1/4 teaspoon dried thyme leaves

1 medium carrot, cut up

1 medium stalk celery with leaves, cut up

1 small onion, cut up

5 peppercorns

3 whole cloves

3 sprigs parsley

1 bay leaf

1. Remove marrow from center of bones. Heat marrow in Dutch oven over low heat until melted, or heat 2 tablespoons vegetable oil until hot. Cook beef shanks over medium heat until brown on both sides.

2. Add water; heat to boiling. Skim foam from broth. Stir in remaining ingredients; heat to boiling. Skim foam from broth; reduce heat to low. Cover and simmer 3 hours.

3. Remove beef from broth. Cool beef about 10 minutes or just until cool enough to handle. Strain broth through cheesecloth-lined sieve; discard vegetables and seasonings.

4. Remove beef from bones. Cut beef into 1/2-inch pieces. Skim fat from broth. Use immediately, or cover and refrigerate broth and beef in separate containers up to 24 hours or freeze for future use.

1 SERVING: Calories 235 (Calories from Fat 80); Fat 9g (Saturated 4g); Cholesterol 50mg; Sodium 440mg; Carbohydrate 19g (Dietary Fiber 3g); Protein 22g

New England Clam Chowder

4 SERVINGS

1/4 cup cut-up bacon or lean salt pork

1 medium onion, chopped (about 1/2 cup)

**2 cans (6 1/2 ounces each) minced clams, drained
and liquid reserved**

1 medium potato, diced (about 2 cups)

Dash of pepper

2 cups milk

1. Cook and stir bacon and onion in 2-quart saucepan over medium heat until bacon is crisp.

2. Add enough water, if necessary, to reserved clam liquid to measure 1 cup. Stir clams, liquid, potato and pepper into onion mixture. Heat to boiling; reduce heat.

3. Cover and boil until potatoes are tender, about 15 minutes. Stir in milk. Heat, stirring occasionally, just until hot (do not boil).

1 SERVING: Calories 215 (Calories from Fat 0); Fat 6g (Saturated 0g); Cholesterol 45mg; Sodium 200mg; Carbohydrate 20g (Dietary Fiber 0g); Protein 20g

Wild Rice Soup

5 SERVINGS

Purchase canned wild rice to save on prep time. A 15-ounce can contains about 2 cups cooked wild rice.

2 tablespoons margarine or butter

2 medium stalks celery, sliced (1 cup)

1 medium carrot, coarsely shredded (1 cup)

1 medium onion, chopped (1/2 cup)

1 small green bell pepper, chopped (1/2 cup)

1/4 cup Original Bisquick mix

1/2 teaspoon salt

1/4 teaspoon pepper

1 cup water

1 can (10 1/2 ounces) condensed chicken broth

1 1/2 cups cooked wild rice

1 cup half-and-half

1/3 cup slivered almonds, toasted

1/4 cup chopped fresh parsley

1. Melt margarine in 3-quart saucepan over medium-high heat. Cook celery, carrot, onion and bell pepper in margarine about 4 minutes, stirring occasionally, until tender.

2. Stir in Bisquick mix, salt and pepper. Stir in water, broth and wild rice. Heat to boiling, stirring frequently; reduce heat to low. Cover and simmer 15 minutes, stirring occasionally.

3. Stir in half-and-half, almonds and parsley. Heat just until hot (do not boil).

1 SERVING: Calories 260 (Calories from Fat 145); Fat 16g (Saturated 5g); Cholesterol 20mg; Sodium 700mg; Carbohydrate 24g (Dietary Fiber 3g); Protein 8g

Wild Rice Soup

Minestrone with Pesto

6 SERVINGS

The great thing about minestrone is that you can use whatever vegetables are in season. White cannellini beans can also be used in place of the kidney beans.

4 cups raw vegetable pieces (carrots, celery, zucchini or yellow summer squash, green beans, cut into 1-inch slices, chopped tomatoes or shelled peas)

1 ounce uncooked spaghetti, broken into 2- to 3-inch pieces, or 1/2 cup uncooked macaroni

1/2 teaspoon dried basil leaves

1/8 teaspoon pepper

1 medium onion, chopped

1 clove garlic, finely chopped

1 can (15 ounces) kidney or garbanzo beans, undrained

2 cans (10 1/2 ounces each) condensed beef broth

2 broth cans (10 1/2 ounces each) water

5 ounces spinach, cut crosswise into 1/4-inch strips

Prepared pesto

Grated Parmesan cheese, if desired

1. Heat all ingredients except spinach, pesto and cheese to boiling in 4-quart Dutch oven; reduce heat.

2. Cover and simmer until vegetables and spaghetti are tender, about 10 minutes. Stir in spinach until wilted. Serve with pesto and, if desired, grated Parmesan cheese.

1 SERVING: Calories 200 (Calories from Fat 80); Fat 9g (Saturated 2g); Cholesterol 2mg; Sodium 800mg; Carbohydrate 24g (Dietary Fiber 6g); Protein 12g

Home-Style Potato Soup

5 SERVINGS

For a bit of variety, stir in 1/8 teaspoon dried thyme leaves with the chicken broth and potatoes. Or turn this soup into a tasty potato-cheese soup. When the soup is hot, gradually stir in 1 1/2 cups shredded Cheddar cheese until melted.

1 can (14 1/2 ounces) chicken broth

3 medium potatoes, cut into large pieces (about 1 pound)

1 1/2 cups milk

1/4 teaspoon salt

1/8 teaspoon pepper

2 medium green onions, thinly sliced

1. Heat chicken broth and potatoes to boiling in 2-quart saucepan over high heat, stirring occasionally. Reduce heat; cover and simmer about 15 minutes or until potatoes are tender.

2. Remove saucepan from heat, but do not drain. Break the potatoes into smaller pieces with the potato masher or large fork. The mixture should still be lumpy.

3. Stir the milk, salt, pepper and green onions into the potato mixture. Heat over medium heat, stirring occasionally until hot but do not boil to prevent curdled appearance.

1 SERVING: Calories 120 (Calories from Fat 20); Fat 2g (Saturated 1g); Cholesterol 5mg; Sodium 530mg; Carbohydrate 19g (Dietary Fiber 1g); Protein 6g

Home-Style Potato Soup

New England Baked Bean Stew

4 SERVINGS

New England baked beans traditionally simmer in the oven for many hours. But this range-top version can be on your table in 30 minutes! Serve with a crusty Italian bread.

1/2 pound boneless skinless chicken breasts, cut into 1/2-inch pieces

1/2 pound fully cooked Polish sausage, cut into 1/2-inch slices

1 can (15 to 16 ounces) great northern beans, rinsed and drained

1 can (15 to 16 ounces) dark red kidney beans, rinsed and drained

1 can (14 1/2 ounces) diced tomatoes with olive oil, garlic and spices, undrained

1 tablespoon packed brown sugar

4 medium green onions, sliced (1/4 cup)

1. Spray 12-inch nonstick skillet with cooking spray; heat over medium-high heat. Cook chicken in skillet 3 to 5 minutes, stirring occasionally, until brown.

2. Stir in remaining ingredients except onions. Cook uncovered over medium-low heat 8 to 10 minutes, stirring occasionally, until chicken is no longer pink in center.

3. Stir in onions. Cook 3 to 5 minutes, stirring occasionally, until onions are crisp-tender.

1 SERVING: Calories 525 (Calories from Fat 170); Fat 19g (Saturated 6g); Cholesterol 65mg; Sodium 1150mg; Carbohydrate 64g (Dietary Fiber 15g); Protein 40g

New England Baked Bean Stew

Chili with Corn Dumplings

Feel free to use either white or yellow cornmeal to make this mildly spicy main dish. You can also use 2 cups of frozen corn instead of the canned corn.

1 1/2 pounds ground beef

1 large onion, chopped (3/4 cup)

1 can (15 1/4 ounces) whole kernel corn, undrained

1 can (14 1/2 ounces) stewed tomatoes, undrained

1 can (16 ounces) tomato sauce

2 tablespoons chili powder

1 teaspoon red pepper sauce

1 1/3 cups Original Bisquick mix

2/3 cup cornmeal

2/3 cup milk

3 tablespoons chopped fresh cilantro or parsley,
    if desired

1. Cook beef and onion in 4-quart Dutch oven over medium heat, stirring occasionally, until beef is brown; drain. Reserve 1/2 cup of the corn. Stir remaining corn with liquid, tomatoes, tomato sauce, chili powder and pepper sauce into beef mixture. Heat to boiling; reduce heat. Cover and simmer 15 minutes.

2. Mix Bisquick and cornmeal. Stir in milk, cilantro and reserved 1/2 cup corn just until moistened.

3. Heat chili to boiling. Drop dough by rounded tablespoonfuls onto chili; reduce heat to low. Cook uncovered 10 minutes. Cover and cook about 10 minutes longer or until dumplings are dry.

1 SERVING: Calories 515 (Calories from Fat 200); Fat 22g (Saturated 8g); Cholesterol 65mg; Sodium 1310mg; Carbohydrate 56g (Dietary Fiber 6g); Protein 29g

Chili with Corn Dumplings

Family-Favorite Stew

6 SERVINGS

Go ahead and substitute ground turkey for the ground beef in this recipe for a tasty new twist.

1 pound ground beef

2 cups water

2 cans (14 1/2 ounces each) diced tomatoes in olive oil, garlic and spices, undrained

1 can (6 ounces) tomato paste

1 bag (16 ounces) frozen carrots, green beans and cauliflower (or other combination)

2 1/4 cups Original Bisquick mix

2/3 cup milk

1 tablespoon chopped fresh parsley

1. Heat oven to 425°F. Cook beef in ovenproof 4-quart Dutch oven over medium heat, stirring occasionally, until brown; drain. Stir in water, tomatoes, tomato paste and vegetables. Heat to boiling, stirring occasionally.

2. Mix Bisquick, milk and parsley until soft dough forms. Drop dough by 6 spoonfuls onto beef mixture; remove from heat.

3. Bake uncovered 20 to 25 minutes or until biscuits are golden brown and stew is bubbly.

1 SERVING: Calories 430 (Calories from Fat 170); Fat 19g (Saturated 6g); Cholesterol 45mg; Sodium 1310mg; Carbohydrate 48g (Dietary Fiber 5g); Protein 22g

Hearty Pork Stew

6 SERVINGS

Parsnips, that root vegetable that looks like a creamy white carrot, have a slightly sweet flavor that goes nicely with pork. However, instead of the parsnips, two more sliced carrots can be used and the stew will be just as colorful and tasty.

1 1/2 pounds boneless pork loin, cut into 1-inch cubes

3 medium carrots, cut into 1/4-inch slices (1 1/2 cups)

1 medium onion, chopped (1/2 cup)

1 box (32 ounces) ready-to-serve chicken broth

2 cups 1/2-inch diced peeled parsnips

1 1/2 cups 1-inch cubes peeled butternut squash

1/2 teaspoon salt

1/2 teaspoon pepper

3 tablespoons all-purpose flour

3 tablespoons margarine or butter, softened

1. Mix all ingredients except flour and margarine in 3 1/2- to 6-quart slow cooker.

2. Cover and cook on low heat setting 6 to 7 hours (or high heat setting 3 to 4 hours) or until pork is no longer pink and vegetables are tender.

3. Mix flour and margarine. Gently stir flour mixture, 1 spoonful at a time, into pork mixture until blended.

4. Cover and cook on high heat setting 30 to 45 minutes, stirring occasionally, until thickened.

1 SERVING: Calories 275 (Calories from Fat 115); Fat 13g (Saturated 4g); Cholesterol 50mg; Sodium 1010mg; Carbohydrate 21g (Dietary Fiber 4g); Protein 23g

Hearty Pork Stew

Meat

Meatball Porcupines

2 SERVINGS

Don't worry—these porcupines won't prick you. The combination of rice and ground beef gives these meatballs the appearance of lots of little porcupines.

1/2 pound ground beef

1/4 cup uncooked rice

1/4 cup milk or water

2 tablespoons chopped onion

1/2 teaspoon salt

1/4 teaspoon celery salt

1/8 teaspoon garlic salt

Dash of pepper

1 tablespoon shortening

1 can (8 ounces) tomato sauce

1/2 cup water

1 1/2 teaspoons Worcestershire sauce

1. Mix beef, rice, milk, onion, salt, celery salt, garlic salt and pepper. Form into 4 medium balls.

2. Fry in melted shortening, turning frequently, until light brown (but not crusty) on all sides. Add tomato sauce, water and Worcestershire sauce. Mix well.

3. Cover; simmer 45 minutes over low heat. Add a small amount of additional water if liquid cooks down too much.

1 SERVING: Calories 440 (Calories from Fat 215); Fat 24g (Saturated 8g); Cholesterol 65mg; Sodium 1630mg; Carbohydrate 32g (Dietary Fiber 2g); Protein 26g

Favorite Meat Loaf

6 SERVINGS

A family favorite, this meat loaf often does double duty. Once, served up with hot mashed or baked potatoes, then cold, served on thick slices of bread. For added flavor, spread the top of the meat loaf before baking with ketchup, barbecue sauce or salsa.

1 pound ground beef

1/2 pound ground pork

1 cup milk

1 tablespoon Worcestershire sauce

1/4 teaspoon pepper

1/4 teaspoon celery salt

1/4 teaspoon garlic salt

1/4 teaspoon ground mustard

1/4 teaspoon ground sage

1 egg, beaten

3 slices white bread, torn into pieces

1 small onion, chopped (1/4 cup)

1. Heat oven to 350°F.

2. Mix all ingredients. Spread in ungreased loaf pan, 9 x 5 x 3 inches.

3. Bake 1 1/2 hours or until beef mixture is no longer pink in center and juice is clear.

4. Let stand 5 minutes; remove from pan.

1 SERVING: Calories 340 (Calories from Fat 170); Fat 19g (Saturated 7g); Cholesterol 105mg; Sodium 370mg; Carbohydrate 17g (Dietary Fiber 1g); Protein 26g

Favorite Meat Loaf

Overnight Lasagna

6 SERVINGS

Lasagna is an American favorite, always perfect for family meals, casual get-togethers and potluck suppers. Even better, you can put this lasagna together the night before and bake it the following day.

1 pound ground beef

1 medium onion, chopped (about 1/2 cup)

1 clove garlic, crushed

1/3 cup chopped fresh or 2 tablespoons dried parsley leaves

1 tablespoon sugar

2 tablespoons chopped fresh or 1 1/2 teaspoons dried basil leaves

1 teaspoon seasoned salt

1 can (16 ounces) whole tomatoes, undrained

1 can (10 3/4 ounces) condensed tomato soup

1 can (6 ounces) tomato paste

2 1/2 cups water

12 uncooked lasagna noodles (about 12 ounces)

1 container (12 ounces) creamed cottage cheese

2 cups shredded mozzarella cheese (8 ounces)

1/4 cup grated Parmesan cheese

1. Cook, stirring, ground beef, onion and garlic in Dutch oven until beef is brown; drain. Stir in parsley, sugar, basil, seasoned salt, tomatoes, tomato soup, tomato paste and water; break up tomatoes.

2. Heat to boiling, stirring occasionally; reduce heat. Simmer uncovered 20 minutes.

3. Spread 2 cups of the sauce mixture in ungreased rectangular baking dish, 13 x 9 x 2 inches. Top with 4 noodles. Spread half of the cottage cheese over noodles; spread with 2 cups of the sauce mixture. Sprinkle with 1 cup of the mozzarella cheese. Repeat with 4 noodles, the remaining cottage cheese, 2 cups of the sauce mixture and the remaining mozzarella cheese. Top with the remaining noodles and sauce mixture; sprinkle with Parmesan cheese. Cover and refrigerate up to 12 hours.

4. Heat oven to 350°F. Bake covered 30 minutes. Uncover and bake until hot and bubbly, 30 to 40 minutes longer. Let stand 15 minutes before cutting.

1 SERVING: Calories 425 (Calories from Fat 155); Fat 17g (Saturated 8g); Cholesterol 55mg; Sodium 1160mg; Carbohydrate 41g (Dietary Fiber 3g); Protein 30g

Savory Spaghetti

A delicious, moist spaghetti dish that is really simple to do. What's even better is that you don't have to boil the spaghetti separately. The noodles and sauce all cook up in one skillet. Now, that's easy!

1/2 pound ground beef

1/4 pound ground pork

1 small onion, chopped

1 small green pepper, sliced

1/2 cup sliced ripe olives

1 can (2 ounces) mushrooms, drained

1 can (8 ounces) tomato sauce

2 1/2 cups tomatoes (1 pound 4 ounces)

2 cups water

2 teaspoons salt

1/4 teaspoon pepper

1 teaspoon Worcestershire sauce

6 drops red pepper sauce

4 ounces long spaghetti or noodles

1. Brown beef and pork in large skillet over medium heat. Add onion and green pepper and cook 5 minutes. Add olives, mushrooms and tomato sauce and mix lightly. Stir mixture of tomatoes, water, salt, pepper, Worcestershire sauce and pepper sauce into meat mixture.

2. Add uncooked spaghetti and bring to boil. Cover tightly, reduce heat to low and simmer about 40 minutes, stirring occasionally. Uncover and simmer 15 minutes longer.

1 SERVING: Calories 275 (Calories from Fat 115); Fat 13g (Saturated 4g); Cholesterol 45mg; Sodium 1230mg; Carbohydrate 25g (Dietary Fiber 3g); Protein 18g

New England Pot Roast

8 SERVINGS

A whole jar of horseradish might sound overpowering to you, but we assure you it adds a nice, savory flavor to this dish without overwhelming your taste buds. The meat and vegetables simmer away in the juices and emerge from the oven tender and flavorful. This roast also makes a great gravy.

4-pound beef arm, blade or cross rib pot roast*

1 to 2 teaspoons salt

1 teaspoon pepper

1 jar (8 ounces) prepared horseradish

1 cup water

8 small potatoes, cut in half

8 medium carrots, cut into fourths

8 small onions

Pot Roast Gravy (right)

1. Cook beef in Dutch oven over medium heat until brown on all sides; reduce heat to low.

2. Sprinkle beef with salt and pepper. Spread horseradish over all sides of beef. Add water to Dutch oven. Heat to boiling; reduce heat to low. Cover and simmer 2 1/2 hours.

3. Add potatoes, carrots and onions. Cover and simmer about 1 hour or until beef and vegetables are tender.

4. Remove beef and vegetables to warm platter; keep warm. Prepare Pot Roast Gravy. Serve with beef and vegetables.

*3-pound beef bottom round, rolled rump, tip or chuck eye roast can be substituted; decrease salt to 3/4 teaspoon.

POT ROAST GRAVY

Water

1/2 cup cold water

1/4 cup all-purpose flour

Skim excess fat from broth in Dutch oven. Add enough water to broth to measure 2 cups. Shake 1/2 cup cold water and the flour in tightly covered container; gradually stir into broth. Heat to boiling, stirring constantly. Boil and stir 1 minute.

1 SERVING: Calories 365 (Calories from Fat 100); Fat 11g (Saturated 4g); Cholesterol 85mg; Sodium 400mg; Carbohydrate 38g (Dietary Fiber 6g); Protein 35g

Caramelized Onion Pot Roast

12 SERVINGS

If you have roast left over, try this idea. Chop the beef. Place 2 cups chopped beef in each freezer or refrigerator container. Add the onions and 1/4 cup beef juices to each container. Cover and refrigerate up to 4 days or freeze up to 4 months. To thaw the frozen beef mixture, place the container in the refrigerator about 8 hours.

4-pound boneless beef chuck roast

1 tablespoon olive or vegetable oil

1 teaspoon salt

1/2 teaspoon pepper

6 medium onions, sliced

1 1/2 cups beef broth

3/4 cup sparkling cider

2 tablespoons packed brown sugar

3 tablespoons Dijon mustard

2 tablespoons cider vinegar

1. Trim excess fat from beef. Heat oil in 10-inch skillet over medium-high heat. Cook beef in oil about 10 minutes, turning occasionally, until brown on all sides. Sprinkle with salt and pepper.

2. Place onions in 3 1/2- to 6-quart slow cooker. Place beef on onions.

3. Mix remaining ingredients; pour over beef and onions. Cover and cook on low heat setting 8 to 10 hours or until beef is tender.

4. Remove beef and onions from cooker, using slotted spoon. Cut beef into slices. Skim fat from beef juices in cooker if desired. Serve beef with juices.

1 SERVING: Calories 205 (Calories from Fat 100); Fat 11g (Saturated 4g); Cholesterol 55mg; Sodium 420mg; Carbohydrate 8g (Dietary Fiber 1g); Protein 20g

Caramelized Onion Pot Roast

Beef and Potatoes with Rosemary

8 SERVINGS

If your family likes gravy, you may want to thicken the beef juices from the slow cooker. Skim the fat from the juices. Measure 1 1/2 cups of the juices; pour into a small saucepan. Heat to boiling over medium-high heat. Shake 2 tablespoons cornstarch and 1/4 cup cold water in a tightly covered jar. Stir the cornstarch mixture into the beef juices. Cook about 5 minutes, stirring occasionally, until thickened.

1 pound medium red potatoes, cut into fourths

1 cup baby-cut carrots

3-pound boneless beef chuck roast

3 tablespoons Dijon mustard

2 tablespoons chopped fresh or 1 1/2 teaspoons dried rosemary leaves, crumbled

1 teaspoon chopped fresh or 1/2 teaspoon dried thyme leaves

1 teaspoon salt

1/2 teaspoon pepper

1 small onion, finely chopped (1/4 cup)

1 1/2 cups beef broth

1. Arrange potatoes and carrots in 3 1/2- to 6-quart slow cooker.

2. Trim excess fat from beef. Mix mustard, rosemary, thyme, salt and pepper; spread evenly over beef. Place beef in cooker. Sprinkle onion over beef. Pour broth evenly over beef and vegetables.

3. Cover and cook on low heat setting 8 to 10 hours or until beef and vegetables are tender.

4. Remove beef and vegetables from cooker, using slotted spoon; place on serving platter. Skim fat from beef juices in cooker if desired. Serve beef with juices.

1 SERVING: Calories 250 (Calories from Fat 110); Fat 12g (Saturated 4g); Cholesterol 60mg; Sodium 550mg; Carbohydrate 14g (Dietary Fiber 2g); Protein 23g

Beef and Potatoes with Rosemary

Beef Brisket Barbecue

12 SERVINGS

The slow-cooking brisket emerges tender and succulent. Any leftovers can be transformed into delicious sandwiches the next day. Or, you can shred the brisket and stir in enough warm barbecue sauce to moisten it. It is delicious as a sandwich or spooned over hot mashed potatoes or rice.

4 to 5 pounds well-trimmed fresh beef brisket (not corned)

1 teaspoon salt

1/2 cup ketchup

1/4 cup white vinegar

1 tablespoon Worcestershire sauce

1 1/2 teaspoons liquid smoke

1/4 teaspoon pepper

1 medium onion, finely chopped (1/2 cup)

1 bay leaf

1. Heat oven to 325°F.

2. Rub surface of beef with salt. Place in ungreased rectangular pan, 18 x 9 x 2 inches. Mix remaining ingredients; pour over beef.

3. Cover and bake about 3 hours or until beef is tender.

4. Cut thin diagonal slices across grain at an angle from 2 or 3 "faces" of beef. Spoon any remaining pan juices over sliced beef if desired. Remove bay leaf.

1 SERVING: Calories 245 (Calories from Fat 100); Fat 11g (Saturated 4g); Cholesterol 85mg; Sodium 390mg; Carbohydrate 4g (Dietary Fiber 0g); Protein 33g

Spicy Pepper Steak Stir-Fry

4 SERVINGS

Chili oil is available in Asian markets or in the Asian foods section of the grocery store. If you don't have chili oil, just add 1/4 teaspoon ground red pepper (cayenne) or 1/2 teaspoon red pepper sauce to 1 tablespoon vegetable oil for the same kick and great flavor.

1 tablespoon chili oil or vegetable oil

1 pound beef strips for stir-fry

1 medium bell pepper, cut into 3/4-inch squares

1 medium onion, sliced

1/4 cup hoisin sauce

Hot cooked noodles or rice, if desired

1. Heat wok or 12-inch skillet over high heat. Add oil; rotate wok to coat side.

2. Add beef; stir-fry about 2 minutes or until brown. Add bell pepper and onion; stir-fry about 1 minute or until vegetables are crisp-tender. Stir in hoisin sauce; cook and stir about 30 seconds or until hot. Serve with noodles.

1 SERVING: Calories 185 (Calories from Fat 65); Fat 7g (Saturated 2g); Cholesterol 55mg; Sodium 40mg; Carbohydrate 9g (Dietary Fiber 1g); Protein 23g

Spicy Pepper Steak Stir-Fry

Classic Beef Stroganoff

8 SERVINGS

This elegant entree, named after a 19th-century Russian diplomat, Count Stroganv, combines a sour cream sauce with tender beef, onions and mushrooms. Don't let the sauce boil once you've added the sour cream or it will curdle.

2 pounds beef sirloin steak, 1/2-inch thick

8 ounces mushrooms, sliced

2 medium onions, thinly sliced

1 clove garlic, finely chopped

1/4 cup margarine or butter

1 1/2 cups beef broth

1 teaspoon salt

1 teaspoon Worcestershire sauce

1/4 cup all-purpose flour

1 1/2 cups sour cream

4 cups hot cooked egg noodles

1. Cut beef steak across grain into strips, 1 1/2 x 1/2 inches.

2. Cook and stir mushrooms, onions and garlic in margarine in 10-inch skillet until onions are tender; remove from skillet. Cook beef in same skillet until brown. Stir in 1 cup of the broth, the salt and the Worcestershire sauce. Heat to boiling; reduce heat. Cover and simmer 15 minutes.

3. Stir remaining 1/2 cup broth into flour; stir into beef mixture. Add onion mixture; heat to boiling, stirring constantly. Boil and stir 1 minute. Stir in sour cream; heat until hot (do not boil). Serve over noodles.

1 SERVING: Calories 385 (Calories from Fat 170); Fat 19g (Saturated 10g); Cholesterol 125mg; Sodium 300mg; Carbohydrate 28g (Dietary Fiber 2g); Protein 27g

Pasta with Beef, Broccoli and Tomatoes

6 SERVINGS

If you can't find radiatore pasta, use any large-size pasta such as mostaccioli, penne, rigatoni or ziti instead. Partially frozen beef can be sliced very easily and evenly—give it a try.

3/4 pound beef boneless sirloin steak

3 cups uncooked radiatore (nuggets) pasta (9 ounces)

1/2 teaspoon pepper

1 package (16 ounces) fresh or frozen broccoli cuts (6 cups)

1 can (14 1/2 ounces) diced tomatoes with roasted garlic, undrained

1 can (14 1/2 ounces) beef broth

2 tablespoons cornstarch

2 tablespoons Worcestershire sauce

1. Trim fat from beef. Cut beef into 1/4-inch strips.

2. Cook and drain pasta as directed on package. While pasta is cooking, spray 12-inch skillet with cooking spray; heat over medium-high heat. Add beef to skillet; sprinkle with pepper. Cook 2 to 3 minutes, stirring frequently, until brown.

3. Stir in broccoli, tomatoes and broth; reduce heat. Cover and simmer about 10 minutes, stirring occasionally, until broccoli is crisp-tender.

4. Mix cornstarch and Worcestershire sauce; stir into beef mixture. Heat to boiling, stirring constantly. Boil and stir 1 minute. Toss beef mixture and pasta.

1 SERVING: Calories 270 (Calories from Fat 30); Fat 3g (Saturated 1g); Cholesterol 30mg; Sodium 500mg; Carbohydrate 44g (Dietary Fiber 4g); Protein 21g

Pasta with Beef, Broccoli and Tomatoes

Savory Beef Tenderloin

4 SERVINGS

Beef tenderloin can be more expensive than regular steak, but it's worth it for the time you'll save cooking. In just a few minutes of sautéing, this beef becomes melt-in-your-mouth tender. For a special occasion dinner, serve with mashed potatoes and steamed green beans.

3/4 pound beef tenderloin

2 teaspoons chopped fresh or 1/2 teaspoon dried marjoram leaves

2 teaspoons sugar

1 teaspoon coarsely ground pepper

1 tablespoon butter or margarine

1 cup sliced mushrooms (3 ounces)

1 small onion, thinly sliced

1 cup beef broth

1 tablespoon cornstarch

1. Cut beef into four 3/4-inch-thick slices. Mix marjoram, sugar and pepper; rub on both sides of beef slices. Melt butter in 10-inch skillet over medium heat. Cook beef in butter 3 to 5 minutes, turning once, until brown. Remove beef to serving platter; keep warm.

2. Cook mushrooms and onion in drippings in skillet over medium heat about 2 minutes, stirring occasionally, until onion is crisp-tender.

3. Mix broth and cornstarch; stir into mushroom mixture. Cook over medium heat, stirring constantly, until mixture thickens and boils. Boil and stir 1 minute. Pour over beef.

1 SERVING: Calories 190 (Calories from Fat 80); Fat 9g (Saturated 4g); Cholesterol 45mg; Sodium 310mg; Carbohydrate 7g (Dietary Fiber 0g); Protein 21g

Beef Rib Roast with Yorkshire Pudding

8 SERVINGS

Take a tip from the English—serve your next rib roast with Yorkshire Pudding. It resembles a little soufflé, puffs up like a popover and tastes like the drippings from the roast that it bakes in. When buying the roast, look for it under several names: beef rib roast, standing rib roast or prime rib roast.

4- to 6-pound beef rib roast (small end)

1/2 teaspoon salt

1/4 teaspoon pepper

Yorkshire Pudding (right)

1. Heat oven to 350°F. For easy cleanup, line shallow roasting pan with foil. Place beef, fat side up, in roasting pan; sprinkle with salt and pepper. Insert ovenproof meat thermometer so tip is in center of the thickest part of beef and does not rest in fat or touch bone. (Do not add water.)

2. *For medium-rare*, bake 1 hour 45 minutes to 2 hours or until thermometer reads 135°F. Remove beef from pan onto carving board. Cover beef loosely with foil and let stand 15 to 20 minutes until thermometer reads 145°F. (Temperature will continue to rise about 10°F, and beef will be easier to carve.) *For medium*, bake uncovered 2 hours to 2 hours 30 minutes or until thermometer reads 150°F. Cover beef loosely with foil and let stand 15 to 20 minutes or until thermometer reads 160°F.

3. While beef is standing, make Yorkshire Pudding. Serve Yorkshire Pudding immediately with beef.

YORKSHIRE PUDDING

Vegetable oil, if necessary

1 cup all-purpose flour

1 cup milk

1/2 teaspoon salt

2 large eggs

Measure pan drippings, adding enough oil to drippings, if necessary, to measure 1/4 cup. Place hot drippings in square pan, 9 x 9 inches; place pan in oven and heat until hot. Increase oven temperature to 450°F. In medium bowl, beat flour, milk, salt and eggs with wire whisk just until smooth. Pour batter into pan of drippings and oil. Bake 18 to 23 minutes or until puffy and golden brown (pudding will puff during baking but will deflate shortly after being removed from oven). Cut pudding into squares.

1 SERVING: Calories 340 (Calories from Fat 155); Fat 17g (Saturated 7g); Cholesterol 135mg; Sodium 390mg; Carbohydrate 14g (Dietary Fiber 0g); Protein 32g

Wild Rice– and Almond-Stuffed Pork Chops

4 SERVINGS

Quick-cooking wild rice is faster to prepare than regular wild rice and is equally delicious. If you can't find wild rice, try a wild rice blend or brown rice instead.

Wild Rice and Almond Stuffing (right)

4 pork loin chops, 1 inch thick (about 2 1/2 pounds)

1/3 cup apricot preserves

1 tablespoon apple juice or water

1/8 teaspoon ground cinnamon

1. Prepare Wild Rice and Almond Stuffing.

2. Cut a deep pocket in each pork chop on the meatiest side of the bone. Press about 1/3 cup stuffing mixture into each pocket. Secure openings with toothpicks. Mix apricot preserves, apple juice and cinnamon.

3. Cover and grill pork 4 to 5 inches from medium-low coals 40 to 45 minutes, brushing occasionally with apricot mixture and turning 2 or 3 times, until pork is no longer pink when cut near bone on the unstuffed sides of chops. Remove toothpicks.

WILD RICE AND ALMOND STUFFING

1/3 cup finely chopped celery

1 green onion, finely chopped

1 teaspoon margarine or butter

1 cup cooked wild rice

1 tablespoon sliced almonds

1/4 teaspoon salt

1/8 teaspoon pepper

Cook celery and onion in margarine in 8-inch skillet over medium heat, stirring frequently, until celery is crisp-tender. Stir in remaining ingredients.

1 SERVING: Calories 430 (Calories from Fat 150); Fat 16g (Saturated 5g); Cholesterol 120mg; Sodium 380mg; Carbohydrate 28g (Dietary Fiber 1g); Protein 43g

Corn Bread– and Bacon-Stuffed Pork Chops

6 SERVINGS

**6 pork rib or loin chops, 1 to 1 1/4 inches thick
(about 4 pounds)**

4 slices bacon, cut into 1/2-inch pieces

1 medium onion, chopped (1/2 cup)

1 small green bell pepper, chopped (1/2 cup)

1 cup corn bread stuffing crumbs

1/2 cup water

1/2 cup shredded Cheddar cheese (2 ounces)

1/2 teaspoon seasoned salt

1/2 teaspoon dried marjoram leaves

1/4 teaspoon pepper

1. Heat oven to 350°F.

2. Make a pocket in each pork chop by cutting into side of chop toward the bone.

3. Cook bacon in 12-inch skillet over medium heat, stirring occasionally, until crisp. Stir in onion and bell pepper. Cook 2 to 3 minutes, stirring occasionally, until vegetables are crisp-tender; remove from heat. Drain. Stir in stuffing crumbs and water until well mixed. Stir in cheese.

4. Sprinkle both sides of pork with seasoned salt, marjoram and pepper. Fill pockets with about 1/3 cup corn bread mixture. Cook pork in same skillet over medium heat, turning once, until brown. Place pork in ungreased rectangular pan, 13 x 9 x 2 inches. Cover tightly with aluminum foil.

5. Bake 45 minutes. Uncover and bake about 15 minutes longer or until pork is slightly pink when cut near bone.

1 SERVING: Calories 335 (Calories from Fat 180); Fat 20g (Saturated 7g); Cholesterol 90mg; Sodium 550mg; Carbohydrate 15g (Dietary Fiber 1g); Protein 25g

Corn Bread– and Bacon-Stuffed Pork Chops

Pork Chop and New Potato Skillet

6 SERVINGS

New potatoes are young potatoes of any variety. If you can't find any new potatoes, use Round Red or Round White instead. If they are large, you might have to cut them into sixths instead of fourths.

6 pork loin or rib chops, 1/2 inch thick (about 1 1/2 pounds)

1 can (10 3/4 ounces) condensed cream of mushroom soup

1 can (4 ounces) mushroom stems and pieces, undrained

1/3 cup water

3/4 teaspoon chopped fresh or 1/4 teaspoon dried thyme leaves

1/2 teaspoon garlic powder

1/2 teaspoon Worcestershire sauce

6 medium new potatoes (about 1 1/2 pounds), cut into fourths

1 tablespoon chopped pimiento

1 package (9 ounces) frozen green peas, rinsed and drained

1. Spray 10-inch nonstick skillet with nonstick cooking spray; heat skillet over medium-high heat. Cook pork in skillet until brown on both sides.

2. Mix soup, mushrooms, water, thyme, garlic powder and Worcestershire sauce; pour over pork. Heat to boiling, stirring occasionally; reduce heat. Cover and simmer 15 minutes.

3. Add potatoes. Cover and simmer 15 minutes. Stir in pimiento and peas. Cover and simmer about 10 minutes, stirring occasionally, until pork is tender and slightly pink when centers of thickest pieces are cut and peas are tender.

1 SERVING: Calories 350 (Calories from Fat 110); Fat 12g (Saturated 4g); Cholesterol 70mg; Sodium 520mg; Carbohydrate 31g (Dietary Fiber 5g); Protein 29g

Pork Chop and New Potato Skillet

Peach- and Mustard-Glazed Pork Tenderloin

6 SERVINGS

1/2 cup peach preserves

2 tablespoons Dijon mustard

2 teaspoons vegetable oil

1/4 teaspoon dried thyme leaves

1/4 teaspoon salt

2 pork tenderloins (about 3/4 pound each)

1. Mix all ingredients except pork. Place pork in resealable plastic food-storage bag or shallow glass or plastic dish. Pour preserves mixture over pork; turn pork to coat with preserves mixture. Seal bag or cover dish and refrigerate at least 1 hour but no longer than 8 hours, turning pork occasionally.

2. Heat oven to 450°F.

3. Remove pork from marinade; reserve marinade in 1-quart saucepan. Place pork in shallow roasting pan. Insert meat thermometer so tip is in thickest part of pork.

4. Bake uncovered 25 to 30 minutes or until thermometer reads 155°F. Cover pork with aluminum foil and let stand 10 to 15 minutes, brushing once with reserved marinade, until thermometer reads 160°F. (Temperature will continue to rise about 5°F, and pork will be easier to carve.)

5. Heat marinade to boiling. Boil 1 minute, stirring constantly. Cut pork into slices. Serve with marinade.

1 SERVING: Calories 220 (Calories from Fat 55); Fat 6g (Saturated 2g); Cholesterol 65mg; Sodium 220mg; Carbohydrate 18g (Dietary Fiber 0g); Protein 24g

Peach- and Mustard-Glazed Pork Tenderloin

Pork Crown Roast

12 SERVINGS

This special roast may be on hand at your supermarket during the holidays, but call the meat department ahead of time to make sure. Those fancy paper frills usually come with the roast.

7 1/2- to 8-pound pork crown roast (about 20 ribs)

2 teaspoons salt

1 teaspoon pepper

1. Sprinkle pork with salt and pepper. Place pork, bone ends up, on rack in shallow roasting pan. Wrap bone ends in foil to prevent excessive browning. Insert meat thermometer so tip is in thickest part of meat and does not touch bone or rest in fat. Place small heatproof bowl or crumpled foil in crown to hold shape of roast evenly. Do not add water. Do not cover.

2. Roast in 350°F oven (preheating oven is not necessary) 2 hours 30 minutes to 3 hours or until thermometer reads 155°F.

3. Remove pork from oven, cover with tent of foil and let stand 15 to 20 minutes or until thermometer reads 160°F. (Temperature will continue to rise about 5°F, and pork will be easier to carve.)

4. Remove foil wrapping; place paper frills on bone ends. To serve, cut pork between ribs.

1 SERVING: Calories 680 (Calories from Fat 250); Fat 28g (Saturated 8g); Cholesterol 110mg; Sodium 1,500mg; Carbohydrate 61g (Dietary Fiber 3g); Protein 49g

Slow-Cooker Garlic Pork Roast

10 SERVINGS

Jazz up your pork roast with more flavor by using chicken broth instead of water and serving with sautéed bell peppers.

3 1/2-pound boneless pork loin roast

1 tablespoon vegetable oil

1 teaspoon salt

1/2 teaspoon pepper

1 medium onion, sliced

3 cloves garlic, peeled

1 cup water

1. Trim excess fat from pork. Heat oil in 10-inch skillet over medium-high heat. Cook pork in oil about 10 minutes, turning occasionally, until brown on all sides. Sprinkle with salt and pepper.

2. Place onion and garlic in 3 1/2- to 6-quart slow cooker. Place pork on onion and garlic. Pour water over pork.

3. Cover and cook on low heat setting 8 to 10 hours or until pork is tender.

1 SERVING: Calories 270 (Calories from Fat 125); Fat 14g (Saturated 5g); Cholesterol 100mg; Sodium 300mg; Carbohydrate 1g (Dietary Fiber 0g); Protein 35g

Slow-Cooker Garlic Pork Roast

Glazed Baked Ham

20 SERVINGS

6-pound fully cooked smoked bone-in ham*

Brown Sugar–Orange Glaze (below) or Pineapple Glaze (right)

1. Heat oven to 325°F. Place ham on rack in shallow roasting pan. Insert meat thermometer in thickest part of ham. Bake uncovered 1 hour 30 minutes or until thermometer reads 135°F to 140°F.

2. Make desired glaze. Brush glaze over ham during last 45 minutes of baking.

3. Remove ham from oven, cover with tent with aluminum foil and let stand 10 to 15 minutes for easier carving.

*Nutrition run calculated on a 6-pound bone-in ham.

BROWN SUGAR–ORANGE GLAZE

1/2 cup packed brown sugar

2 tablespoons orange or pineapple juice

1/2 teaspoon ground mustard

Mix all ingredients.

PINEAPPLE GLAZE

1 cup packed brown sugar

1 tablespoon cornstarch

1/4 teaspoon salt

1 can (8 ounces) crushed pineapple in syrup, undrained

2 tablespoons lemon juice

1 tablespoon yellow mustard

Mix brown sugar, cornstarch and salt in 1-quart saucepan. Stir in pineapple, lemon juice and mustard. Cook over medium heat, stirring constantly, until mixture thickens and boils. Boil and stir 1 minute.

1 SERVING: Calories 125 (Calories from Fat 35); Fat 4g (Saturated 1g); Cholesterol 40mg; Sodium 890mg; Carbohydrate 7g (Dietary Fiber 0g); Protein 15g

Ham and Scalloped Potatoes

6 SERVINGS

You might want to make this recipe using unpeeled potatoes for some added nutrition and flavor. The few extra minutes you use scrubbing the potatoes will be worth it!

**6 medium boiling or baking potatoes (2 pounds),
   peeled**

3 tablespoons margarine or butter

1 small onion, finely chopped (1/4 cup)

3 tablespoons all-purpose flour

1 teaspoon salt

1/4 teaspoon pepper

2 1/2 cups milk

1 1/2 cups diced fully cooked ham

1 tablespoon margarine or butter

1. Heat oven to 350°F. Grease 2-quart casserole.

2. Cut potatoes into enough thin slices to measure about 4 cups.

3. Melt 3 tablespoons margarine in 2-quart saucepan over medium heat. Cook onion in margarine about 2 minutes, stirring occasionally, until tender. Stir in flour, salt and pepper. Cook, stirring constantly, until smooth and bubbly; remove from heat.

4. Stir milk into sauce. Heat to boiling, stirring constantly. Boil and stir 1 minute. Stir in ham.

5. Spread potatoes in casserole. Pour sauce over potatoes. Dot with 1 tablespoon margarine.

6. Cover and bake 30 minutes. Uncover and bake 1 hour to 1 hour 10 minutes longer or until potatoes are tender. Let stand 5 to 10 minutes before serving.

1 SERVING: Calories 295 (Calories from Fat 115); Fat 13g (Saturated 4g); Cholesterol 25mg; Sodium 1040mg; Carbohydrate 33g (Dietary Fiber 2g); Protein 13g

Ham and Scalloped Potatoes

CHAPTER 5

Poultry

Fried Chicken and Creamy Gravy

6 SERVINGS

Fried chicken used to be the Sunday dinner of choice for many Southern families. Most cooks swear by a heavy cast-iron skillet for frying chicken, to make it crisp on the outside, moist and tender on the inside. If you don't have a cast-iron skillet, a heavy enameled Dutch oven will do well, too.

1/2 cup all-purpose flour

1 teaspoon salt

1 teaspoon paprika

1/4 teaspoon pepper

2 1/2- to 3-pound cut-up broiler-fryer chicken

Vegetable oil

Creamy Gravy (right)

1. Mix flour, salt, paprika and pepper. Coat chicken with flour mixture.

2. Heat oil (1/4 inch) in 12-inch skillet over medium-high heat until hot. Cook chicken in oil until light brown on all sides, about 10 minutes; reduce heat. Cover tightly and simmer, turning once or twice, until thickest pieces are done and juices of chicken run clear, about 35 minutes. If skillet cannot be covered tightly, add 1 to 2 tablespoons water.

3. Remove cover during the last 5 minutes of cooking to crisp chicken. Remove chicken; keep warm. Prepare Creamy Gravy; serve with chicken.

CREAMY GRAVY

1 tablespoon all-purpose flour

1/2 cup chicken broth or water

1/2 cup milk

Few drops browning sauce, if desired

Salt and pepper to taste

Pour drippings from skillet into bowl, leaving brown particles in skillet. Return 2 tablespoons drippings to skillet. Stir in flour. Cook over low heat, stirring constantly, until smooth and bubbly; remove from heat. Stir in broth and milk. Heat to boiling, stirring constantly. Boil and stir 1 minute. Stir in browning sauce. Stir in salt and pepper.

1 SERVING: Calories 310 (Calories from Fat 170); Fat 19g (Saturated 4g); Cholesterol 70mg; Sodium 710mg; Carbohydrate 10g (Dietary Fiber 0g); Protein 25g

Baked Barbecued Chicken

6 SERVINGS

Barbecued chicken is a year-round favorite. Serve with a side of mashed potatoes, coleslaw or corn bread to make this best-loved recipe a best-loved meal.

1/4 cup margarine or butter

2 1/2- to 3-pound cut-up broiler-fryer chicken

1 cup ketchup

1/2 cup water

1/4 cup lemon juice

1 tablespoon Worcestershire sauce

2 teaspoons paprika

1/2 teaspoon salt

1 medium onion, finely chopped (about 1/2 cup)

1 clove garlic, finely chopped

1. Heat oven to 375°F.

2. Heat margarine in rectangular pan, 13 x 9 x 2 inches, in oven. Place chicken in margarine, turning to coat. Arrange skin side down in pan. Bake uncovered 30 minutes.

3. Mix remaining ingredients in 1-quart saucepan. Heat to boiling; remove from heat. Drain fat from chicken; turn skin side up. Spoon sauce over chicken. Bake uncovered until thickest pieces are done and juices of chicken run clear, about 30 minutes longer.

1 SERVING: Calories 315 (Calories from Fat 170); Fat 19g (Saturated 4g); Cholesterol 70mg; Sodium 710mg; Carbohydrate 10g (Dietary Fiber 1g); Protein 23g

Baked Barbecued Chicken

Chicken Cacciatore

6 SERVINGS

Slash time from the preparation of this dish by using 2 cups of your favorite prepared spaghetti sauce for the whole tomatoes, tomato sauce, oregano, basil and salt.

3- to 3 1/2-pound cut-up broiler-fryer chicken

1/2 cup all-purpose flour

1/4 cup vegetable oil

1 medium green bell pepper

2 medium onions

2 cloves garlic, crushed

1 can (16 ounces) whole tomatoes, drained

1 can (8 ounces) tomato sauce

1 cup sliced mushrooms (3 ounces)*

1 1/2 teaspoons chopped fresh or 1/2 teaspoon dried
    oregano leaves

1 teaspoon chopped fresh or 1/4 teaspoon dried
    basil leaves

1/2 teaspoon salt

Grated Parmesan cheese

1. Coat chicken with flour.

2. Heat oil in 12-inch skillet over medium-high heat. Cook chicken in oil 15 to 20 minutes or until brown on all sides; drain.

3. Cut bell pepper and onions crosswise in half; cut each half into fourths. Stir bell pepper, onions and remaining ingredients except cheese into chicken in skillet, breaking up tomatoes. Heat to boiling; reduce heat. Cover and simmer 30 to 40 minutes or until juice of chicken is clear when centers of thickest pieces are cut. Serve with cheese.

*1 can (4 ounces) sliced mushrooms, drained, can be substituted for the fresh mushrooms.

1 SERVING: Calories 330 (Calories from Fat 145); Fat 16g (Saturated 4g); Cholesterol 75mg; Sodium 730mg; Carbohydrate 19g (Dietary Fiber 3g); Protein 30g

Chicken with Mushrooms

4 SERVINGS

Dovetail your tasks by cooking pasta or rice while the chicken cooks. Then, round out your dinner with easy additions like cucumber slices and red or green grapes.

4 boneless skinless chicken breasts
   (about 1 1/4 pounds)
1/4 cup all-purpose flour
1/4 teaspoon salt
1/4 teaspoon pepper
2 tablespoons olive or vegetable oil
2 cloves garlic, finely chopped
1/4 cup chopped fresh parsley or 1 tablespoon
   parsley flakes
1 cup sliced mushrooms (3 ounces)
1/2 cup chicken broth
Hot cooked pasta, if desired

1. Flatten each chicken breast half to 1/4-inch thickness by gently pounding between sheets of plastic wrap or waxed paper. Mix flour, salt and pepper. Coat chicken with flour mixture; shake off excess flour.

2. Heat oil in 10-inch skillet over medium-high heat. Cook garlic and parsley in oil 5 minutes, stirring frequently.

3. Add chicken to skillet. Cook, turning once, until brown. Add mushrooms and chicken broth. Cook 8 to 10 minutes, turning chicken once, until chicken is no longer pink in center. Serve with pasta.

1 SERVING: Calories 255 (Calories from Fat 90); Fat 10g (Saturated 2g); Cholesterol 75mg; Sodium 220mg; Carbohydrate 9g (Dietary Fiber 1g); Protein 28g

Chicken with Mushrooms

Thai Chicken

The flavors of peanut butter, tomato and hot chiles are a popular Thai combination. We took a shortcut and used hot salsa for the tomatoes and chiles. For an equally tasty dish with a little less kick, use a milder salsa.

8 chicken thighs (about 2 pounds), skin removed

3/4 cup hot salsa

1/4 cup peanut butter

2 tablespoons lime juice

1 tablespoon soy sauce

1 teaspoon grated fresh gingerroot

1/4 cup chopped peanuts

2 tablespoons chopped fresh cilantro

1. Place chicken in 3 1/2- to 6-quart slow cooker. Mix remaining ingredients except peanuts and cilantro; pour over chicken.

2. Cover and cook on low heat setting 8 to 9 hours or until juice of chicken is clear when centers of thickest pieces are cut. Remove chicken from cooker, using slotted spoon; place on serving platter.

3. Remove fat from sauce. Pour sauce over chicken. Sprinkle with peanuts and cilantro.

1 SERVING: Calories 380 (Calories from Fat 215); Fat 24g (Saturated 6g); Cholesterol 85mg; Sodium 550mg; Carbohydrate 8g (Dietary Fiber 3g); Protein 36g

Sweet-and-Sour Chicken

Take advantage of packages of precut vegetables for stir-fry or self-serve bins of cut-up raw vegetables, such as broccoli, cauliflower, carrots and celery, in the produce aisle.

1 tablespoon vegetable oil

1 pound boneless skinless chicken breasts, cut into 1-inch pieces

3 cups assorted cut-up vegetables (bell pepper, carrots, tomatoes)

1 can (8 ounces) pineapple chunks in juice, drained

1/2 cup sweet-and-sour sauce

Hot cooked rice or chow mein noodles, if desired

1. Heat wok or 12-inch skillet over high heat. Add oil; rotate wok to coat side.

2. Add chicken; stir-fry about 3 minutes or until no longer pink in center. Add vegetables; stir-fry about 2 minutes or until crisp-tender. Stir in pineapple and sweet-and-sour sauce; cook and stir 1 minute. Serve with rice.

1 SERVING: Calories 215 (Calories from Fat 55); Fat 6g (Saturated 2g); Cholesterol 45mg; Sodium 150mg; Carbohydrate 23g (Dietary Fiber 2g); Protein 19g

Sweet-and-Sour Chicken

Grilled Lemon Chicken

Lemon and chicken go together so well. The lemon adds a nice flavor to the chicken and keeps the meat juicy and tender.

2 1/2- to 3-pound broiler-fryer chicken, cut up

1/2 cup apple juice

1/4 cup lemon juice

2 tablespoons vegetable oil

1 teaspoon paprika

1 lemon, thinly sliced

1 clove garlic, crushed

1 lemon, thinly sliced

Paprika

1. Place chicken in glass or plastic bowl. Mix remaining ingredients except 1 lemon and paprika; pour over chicken. Cover and refrigerate at least 3 hours.

2. Remove chicken and lemon slices. Discard lemon slices; reserve marinade. Cover and grill chicken, bone sides down, 5 to 6 inches from medium coals 15 to 20 minutes; turn chicken. Cover and grill, turning and brushing 2 or 3 times with marinade, until chicken is done, 20 to 40 minutes longer.

3. Roll edges of remaining lemon slices in paprika; arrange around chicken. Garnish with celery leaves if desired.

1 SERVING: Calories 250 (Calories from Fat 140); Fat 16g (Saturated 4g); Cholesterol 70mg; Sodium 70mg; Carbohydrate 4g (Dietary Fiber 0g); Protein 22g

Chicken and Rice Bake

Spanish rice and a green salad tossed with jicama sticks and orange segments make tasty accompaniments to this Mexican specialty.

1 box (6 ounces) original long-grain and wild rice mix

3- to 3 1/2-pound cut-up broiler-fryer chicken, skinned if desired

2 medium stalks celery, sliced (1 cup)

1 jar (4 1/2 ounces) whole mushrooms, drained

2 cups water

1 can (10 3/4 ounces) condensed cream of chicken or cream of celery soup

Paprika

1. Heat oven to 350°F. Spray rectangular baking dish, 13 x 9 x 2 inches, with cooking spray. Pour uncooked rice from rice mix evenly into baking dish. Sprinkle seasoning mix from rice mix evenly over rice. Arrange chicken over rice; arrange celery and mushrooms around chicken.

2. Mix water and soup in 2-quart saucepan; heat to boiling. Pour soup mixture evenly over chicken and vegetables. Sprinkle with paprika. Cover with foil.

3. Bake 1 hour; remove foil. Bake 20 to 30 minutes longer or until juice of chicken is no longer pink when centers of thickest pieces are cut. Let stand 5 minutes before serving.

1 SERVING: Calories 390 (Calories from Fat 150); Fat 17g (Saturated 5g); Cholesterol 95mg; Sodium 910mg; Carbohydrate 26g (Dietary Fiber 1g); Protein 33g

Chicken and Dumplings

4 SERVINGS

1 1/2 cups milk

1 cup frozen peas and carrots

1 cup cut-up cooked chicken

1 can (10 3/4 ounces) condensed cream of chicken
and mushroom soup

1 cup Original Bisquick mix

1/3 cup milk

Paprika, if desired

1. Heat 1 1/2 cups milk, the peas and carrots,
   chicken and soup to boiling in 3-quart saucepan.

2. Stir Bisquick mix and 1/3 cup milk until soft
   dough forms. Drop dough by 8 spoonfuls onto
   chicken mixture; reduce heat to low.

3. Cook uncovered 10 minutes. Cover and cook 10
   minutes longer. Sprinkle with paprika.

1 SERVING: Calories 315 (Calories from Fat 115); Fat 13g
(Saturated 4g); Cholesterol 40mg; Sodium 1070mg;
Carbohydrate 33g (Dietary Fiber 2g); Protein 18g

Chicken and Dumplings

Stuffed Chicken Breasts

4 SERVINGS

Stuffing chicken breasts is a beautiful way to dress up chicken. Not only do the stuffings add color, they are delicious as well!

4 chicken breasts (about 1 1/4 pounds)

Apple-Hazelnut Stuffing (right)

1/2 teaspoon salt

1/4 teaspoon pepper

2 teaspoons margarine or butter, melted

1. Heat oven to 375°F. Grease square pan, 9 x 9 x 2 inches, with shortening.

2. Remove bones from chicken breasts. Do not remove skin.

3. Loosen skin from chicken breasts.

4. Prepare Apple-Hazelnut Stuffing.

5. Spread one-fourth of the stuffing evenly between meat and skin of each chicken breast. Smooth skin over breasts, tucking under loose areas. Place chicken, skin sides up, in pan. Sprinkle with salt and pepper. Drizzle with margarine.

6. Bake uncovered 45 to 55 minutes or until juice of chicken is clear when centers of thickest pieces are cut.

APPLE-HAZELNUT STUFFING

1/4 cup chopped hazelnuts

1 medium apple, chopped (1 cup)

1 package (3 ounces) cream cheese, softened

Mix all ingredients.

1 SERVING: Calories 330 (Calories from Fat 190); Fat 21g (Saturated 7g); Cholesterol 95mg; Sodium 440mg; Carbohydrate 7g (Dietary Fiber 1g); Protein 29g

Pesto Ravioli with Chicken

4 SERVINGS

Looking for something different for dinner? The kids might like this dish topped with a pat of butter and some extra grated cheese. It is a meal everyone will love.

2 teaspoons olive or vegetable oil

1 package (15 ounces) chicken tenders

3/4 cup chicken broth

1 package (9 ounces) refrigerated cheese-filled ravioli

3 small zucchini, cut into 1/4-inch slices

1 large red bell pepper, thinly sliced

1/4 cup refrigerated pesto

Freshly grated Parmesan cheese, if desired

1. Heat oil in 12-inch skillet over medium-high heat. Cook chicken in oil about 4 minutes, turning occasionally, until brown. Remove chicken from skillet.

2. Add broth and ravioli to same skillet. Heat to boiling; reduce heat. Cover and simmer about 4 minutes or until ravioli is tender. Stir in zucchini, bell pepper and chicken. Cook over medium-high heat about 3 minutes, stirring occasionally, until vegetables are crisp-tender and chicken is no longer pink in center. Toss with pesto. Sprinkle with cheese.

1 SERVING: Calories 370 (Calories from Fat 180); Fat 20g (Saturated 6g); Cholesterol 125mg; Sodium 760mg; Carbohydrate 16g (Dietary Fiber 2g); Protein 33g

Pesto Ravioli with Chicken

Ranch Chicken

4 SERVINGS

Keep it simple—pick up a marinated vegetable salad from the grocery deli and brownies from the grocery bakery to complete your meal. For an added treat, top each brownie with a scoop of ice cream and a dollop of chocolate sauce.

4 boneless skinless chicken breasts (about 1/4 pound each)

1/4 cup ranch dressing

1/3 cup seasoned dry bread crumbs

2 tablespoons olive or vegetable oil

1. Remove fat from chicken.

2. Pour the dressing into a shallow bowl or pie pan. Place the bread crumbs on waxed paper or a plate.

3. Dip chicken, one piece at a time, into dressing, coating all sides. Then coat all sides with bread crumbs.

4. Heat oil in 10- or 12-inch skillet over medium-high heat. Cook chicken in oil 12 to 15 minutes, turning once, until golden brown and juice is clear when the centers of the thickest pieces are cut.

1 SERVING: Calories 290 (Calories from Fat 145); Fat 16g (Saturated 3g); Cholesterol 80mg; Sodium 290mg; Carbohydrate 8g (Dietary Fiber 0g); Protein 28g

Easy Chicken Pot Pie

6 SERVINGS

1 cup cut-up cooked chicken

1 bag (16 ounces) frozen peas and carrots, thawed

1 can (10 3/4 ounces) condensed cream of chicken soup

1 cup Original Bisquick mix

1/2 cup milk

1 egg

1. Heat oven to 400°F. Stir chicken, vegetables and soup in ungreased 2-quart casserole.

2. Stir remaining ingredients until blended. Pour over chicken mixture.

3. Bake uncovered about 30 minutes or until crust is golden brown.

1 SERVING: Calories 200 (Calories from Fat 80); Fat 9g (Saturated 3g); Cholesterol 60mg; Sodium 730mg; Carbohydrate 19g (Dietary Fiber 1g); Protein 11g

Easy Chicken Pot Pie

Turkey Divan

6 SERVINGS

Don't wait until you have Thanksgiving leftovers to make this recipe! Use 6 large slices of turkey (about 1/4 inch thick) from the deli. This is also wonderful with fresh asparagus spears in place of the broccoli.

1 1/2 pounds broccoli*

1/4 cup margarine or butter

1/4 cup all-purpose flour

1/8 teaspoon ground nutmeg

1 1/2 cups chicken broth

1/2 cup grated Parmesan cheese

1/2 cup whipping (heavy) cream

6 large slices cooked turkey breast, 1/4 inch thick

    (3/4 pound)

1/2 cup grated Parmesan cheese

1. Prepare and cook broccoli until crisp-tender.

2. Melt margarine in 1-quart saucepan over medium heat. Stir in flour and nutmeg. Cook, stirring constantly, until smooth and bubbly; remove from heat. Stir in broth. Heat to boiling, stirring constantly. Boil and stir 1 minute; remove from heat. Stir in 1/2 cup cheese.

3. Beat whipping cream in chilled small bowl on high speed until stiff. Fold cheese sauce into whipped cream.

4. Place hot broccoli in ungreased rectangular baking dish, 11 x 7 x 1 1/2 inches. Top with turkey. Pour cheese sauce over turkey. Sprinkle with 1/2 cup cheese.

5. Set oven control to Broil.

6. Broil with top 3 to 5 inches from heat, about 3 minutes, or until cheese is bubbly and light brown.

*2 packages (10 ounces each) frozen broccoli spears, cooked and drained, can be substituted for the fresh broccoli.

1 SERVING: Calories 330 (Calories from Fat 180); Fat 20g (Saturated 9g); Cholesterol 85mg; Sodium 710mg; Carbohydrate 10g (Dietary Fiber 2g); Protein 28g

Turkey Tetrazzini

6 SERVINGS

Here's a tasty way to get only 13 grams fat and 390 calories per serving and keep the flavor and creaminess. Use 2 teaspoons chicken bouillon granules and 4 cups evaporated skimmed milk for the chicken broth and half-and-half. Then, decrease the flour to 1/4 cup, the margarine to 2 tablespoons and the almonds to 1/4 cup. Top with reduced-fat Cheddar cheese. Yum!

1 package (7 ounces) spaghetti

2 cups chicken or turkey broth

2 cups half-and-half or milk

1/2 cup all-purpose flour

1/4 cup margarine or butter

1/2 teaspoon salt

1/4 teaspoon pepper

2 cups cut-up cooked turkey or chicken

1 cup sliced ripe olives

1/2 cup slivered almonds

1 cup shredded Cheddar cheese (4 ounces)

1. Heat oven to 350°F. Cook and drain spaghetti as directed on package.

2. Mix broth, half-and-half, flour, margarine, salt and pepper in 3-quart saucepan. Heat to boiling over medium heat, stirring constantly. Boil and stir 1 minute.

3. Stir in spaghetti, turkey, olives and almonds. Spread in ungreased 2-quart casserole. Sprinkle with cheese.

4. Bake uncovered 25 to 30 minutes or until hot and bubbly.

1 SERVING: Calories 590 (Calories from Fat 315); Fat 35g (Saturated 13g); Cholesterol 85mg; Sodium 1030mg; Carbohydrate 42g (Dietary Fiber 3g); Protein 30g

Turkey Tetrazzini

Honey-Mustard Turkey with Snap Peas

4 SERVINGS

Use chicken breast slices rather than turkey if that's what you have on hand. Any of the turkey recipes in this book will work equally well with chicken.

1 pound uncooked turkey breast slices, about
1/4 inch thick
1/2 cup Dijon and honey poultry and meat marinade
1 cup baby-cut carrots, cut lengthwise in half
2 cups frozen snap pea pods (from 1-pound bag)

1. Place turkey in shallow glass or plastic dish. Pour marinade over turkey; turn slices to coat evenly. Cover dish and let stand 10 minutes at room temperature.

2. Spray 10-inch skillet with cooking spray; heat over medium heat. Drain most of marinade from turkey. Cook turkey in skillet about 5 minutes, turning once, until brown.

3. Add carrots, lifting turkey to place carrots on bottom of skillet. Top turkey with pea pods. Cover and simmer about 7 minutes or until carrots are tender and turkey is no longer pink in center.

1 SERVING: Calories 150 (Calories from Fat 10); Fat 1g (Saturated 0g); Cholesterol 75mg; Sodium 65mg; Carbohydrate 9g (Dietary Fiber 3g); Protein 29g

Honey-Mustard Turkey with Snap Peas

Wild Rice and Turkey Casserole

6 SERVINGS

2 cups cut-up cooked turkey

2 1/4 cups boiling water

1/3 cup milk

1 small onion, chopped (1/4 cup)

1 can (10 3/4 ounces) condensed cream of
    mushroom soup

1 package (6 ounces) seasoned long grain and
    wild rice

1. Heat oven to 350°F.

2. Mix all ingredients, including seasoning packet
   from rice mix, in ungreased 2-quart casserole.

3. Cover and bake 45 to 50 minutes or until rice is
   tender. Uncover and bake 10 to 15 minutes
   longer or until liquid is absorbed.

1 SERVING: Calories 155 (Calories from Fat 45); Fat 5g
(Saturated 2g); Cholesterol 40mg; Sodium 500mg; Carbohydrate
12g (Dietary Fiber 0g); Protein 16g

Wild Rice and Turkey Casserole

Orange- and Ginger-Glazed Turkey Tenderloins

4 SERVINGS

This turkey is perfect served with rice, which cooks in about the same amount of time. Follow package directions for cooking the rice. By starting the turkey and rice at the same time, you'll be ready to eat in just 30 minutes, from beginning to end!

1 tablespoon vegetable oil

1 1/4 pounds turkey breast tenderloins

1/3 cup orange marmalade

1 teaspoon finely chopped gingerroot or
   1/2 teaspoon ground ginger

1 teaspoon white or regular Worcestershire sauce

1. Heat oil in 10-inch skillet over medium heat. Cook turkey in oil about 5 minutes or until brown on one side; turn turkey.

2. Stir in remaining ingredients; reduce heat to low.

3. Cover and simmer 15 to 20 minutes, stirring occasionally, until sauce is thickened and juice of turkey is clear when center of thickest piece is cut. Cut turkey into thin slices. Spoon sauce over turkey.

1 SERVING: Calories 365 (Calories from Fat 35); Fat 4g (Saturated 1g); Cholesterol 95mg; Sodium 85mg; Carbohydrate 17g (Dietary Fiber 0g); Protein 33g

Turkey Breast Stuffed with Wild Rice and Cranberries

10 SERVINGS

If you have turkey left over, try this idea. Remove stuffing from turkey. Chop turkey and mix with stuffing. Divide mixture among freezer or refrigerator containers, placing 2 cups in each. Cover and refrigerate up to 4 days or freeze up to 4 months. To thaw frozen turkey mixture, place container in refrigerator about 8 hours.

4 cups cooked wild rice

3/4 cup finely chopped onion

1/2 cup dried cranberries

1/3 cup slivered almonds

2 medium peeled or unpeeled cooking apples, coarsely chopped (2 cups)

4- to 5-pound boneless whole turkey breast, thawed if frozen

1. Mix all ingredients except turkey. Cut turkey into slices at 1-inch intervals about three-fourths of the way through, forming deep pockets.

2. Place turkey in 3 1/2- to 6-quart slow cooker. Stuff pockets with wild rice mixture. Place remaining rice mixture around edge of cooker.

3. Cover and cook on low heat setting 8 to 9 hours or until turkey is no longer pink in center.

1 SERVING: Calories 400 (Calories from Fat 125); Fat 14g (Saturated 3g); Cholesterol 115mg; Sodium 100mg; Carbohydrate 26g (Dietary Fiber 4g); Protein 47g

Turkey Breast Stuffed with Wild Rice and Cranberries

CHAPTER 6

Fish & Seafood

Crispy Baked Fish with Tropical Fruit Salsa

4 SERVINGS

Take a trip to the tropics by serving this dish with couscous or rice that has been cooked in canned coconut milk instead of water.

Tropical Fruit Salsa (right)

3 tablespoons margarine or butter

2/3 cup Original Bisquick mix

1/4 cup yellow cornmeal

1 teaspoon chili powder

1 1/4 teaspoons salt

1 pound orange roughy fillets or other
   white fish fillets

1 egg, beaten

1. Make Tropical Fruit Salsa. Heat oven to 425°F. Melt margarine in rectangular pan, 13 x 9 x 2 inches, in oven.

2. Mix Bisquick, cornmeal, chili powder and salt. Dip fish into egg, then coat with Bisquick mixture. Place in pan.

3. Bake uncovered 10 minutes; turn fish. Bake about 15 minutes longer or until fish flakes easily with fork. Serve with salsa.

TROPICAL FRUIT SALSA

1 cup pineapple chunks

1 tablespoon finely chopped red onion

1 tablespoon chopped fresh cilantro

2 tablespoons lime juice

2 kiwifruit, peeled and chopped

1 mango, cut lengthwise in half, pitted and chopped

1 papaya, peeled, seeded and chopped

1 jalapeño chile, seeded and finely chopped

Mix all ingredients in glass or plastic bowl. Cover and refrigerate at least 1 hour to blend flavors.

1 SERVING: Calories 400 (Calories from Fat 110); Fat 12g (Saturated 2g); Cholesterol 100mg; Sodium 1070mg; Carbohydrate 51g (Dietary Fiber 5g); Protein 27g

Crispy Baked Fish with Tropical Fruit Salsa

Halibut-Asparagus Stir-Fry

4 SERVINGS

Does fresh asparagus sound good? No need to peel the stalks—just break off the tough ends as far down as necessary because the stalks snap easily—and wash them well. Cut the stalks into 1-inch pieces and cook in the same manner as the frozen asparagus.

1 pound halibut, swordfish or tuna fillets, cut into
    1-inch pieces

1 medium onion, thinly sliced

3 cloves garlic, finely chopped

1 teaspoon finely chopped gingerroot

1 box (10 ounces) frozen asparagus cuts, thawed
    and drained

1 package (8 ounces) sliced mushrooms (3 cups)

1 medium tomato, cut into thin wedges

2 tablespoons reduced-sodium soy sauce

1 tablespoon lemon juice

1. Spray 10-inch nonstick skillet with cooking spray; heat over medium-high heat. Add fish, onion, garlic, gingerroot and asparagus; stir-fry 2 to 3 minutes or until fish almost flakes with fork.

2. Carefully stir in remaining ingredients. Cook until heated through and fish flakes easily with fork. Serve with additional soy sauce if desired.

1 SERVING: Calories 140 (Calories from Fat 20); Fat 2g (Saturated 0g); Cholesterol 50mg; Sodium 350mg; Carbohydrate 11g (Dietary Fiber 3g); Protein 22g

Halibut-Asparagus Stir-Fry

Sole Amandine

6 SERVINGS

A French term, amandine means "garnished with almonds" and is often misspelled as "almondine." A shallow oval-shaped baking dish (au gratin dish) also can be used to bake this classic dish.

1 1/2 pounds sole, orange roughy or other delicate fish fillets, about 3/4 inch thick

1/2 cup sliced almonds

1/4 cup butter or margarine, softened

2 tablespoons grated lemon peel

1/2 teaspoon salt

1/2 teaspoon paprika

2 tablespoons lemon juice

1. Heat oven to 375°F. Spray rectangular baking dish, 11 x 7 x 1 1/2 inches, with cooking spray.

2. Cut fish into 6 serving pieces. Place in baking dish. If fish has skin, place skin sides down. Tuck under any thin ends for more even cooking.

3. Mix almonds, butter, lemon peel, salt and paprika; spoon over fish. Sprinkle with lemon juice.

4. Bake uncovered 15 to 20 minutes or until fish flakes easily with fork.

1 SERVING: Calories 180 (Calories from Fat 100); Fat 11g (Saturated 2g); Cholesterol 45mg; Sodium 350mg; Carbohydrate 2g (Dietary Fiber 1g); Protein 19g

Panfried Fish Fillets

6 SERVINGS

Nothing fishy about what to use here! Use any mild-flavored fish that's available, such as flounder, cod, catfish, snapper or halibut.

1 1/2 pounds mild-flavor fish fillets, about 3/4 inch thick

1/2 teaspoon salt

1/8 teaspoon pepper

1 egg

1 tablespoon water

1/2 cup all-purpose flour, cornmeal or grated Parmesan cheese

Vegetable oil or shortening

1. Cut fish fillets into 6 serving pieces. Sprinkle both sides of fish with salt and pepper.

2. Beat egg and water in shallow bowl until well mixed. Sprinkle flour on waxed paper or a plate. Dip both sides of fish pieces into egg, then coat completely with flour.

3. Heat oil (1/8 inch) in 10-inch skillet over medium heat about 2 minutes. Fry fish in oil 6 to 10 minutes, turning once, until fish flakes easily with fork and is brown on both sides. Drain on paper towels.

1 SERVING: Calories 155 (Calories from Fat 55); Fat 6g (Saturated 1g); Cholesterol 80mg; Sodium 90mg; Carbohydrate 5g (Dietary Fiber 0g); Protein 20g

Broiled Salmon with Hazelnut Butter

4 SERVINGS

Salmon and hazelnuts are both native to—and favorites of—the Pacific Northwest. Fresh king salmon, largest of the Pacific salmon, and silver salmon, with its deep coral color, are especially prized. You'll find the delicate Hazelnut Butter a wonderful topping for fish, vegetables and poultry.

Hazelnut Butter (below)

4 salmon fillets (1 to 1 1/2 pounds)

1/2 teaspoon salt

1/8 teaspoon pepper

1. Prepare Hazelnut Butter.

2. Set oven control to Broil. Grease shallow roasting pan or jelly roll pan, 15 1/2 x 10 1/2 x 1 inch.

3. Sprinkle both sides of fish with salt and pepper. Place in pan. Broil fish with tops 4 to 6 inches from heat 4 minutes; turn and spread each fillet with about 1 tablespoon Hazelnut Butter. Broil until fish flakes easily with fork, 4 to 8 minutes.

HAZELNUT BUTTER

2 tablespoons finely chopped hazelnuts

3 tablespoons margarine or butter, softened

1 tablespoon chopped fresh parsley

1 teaspoon lemon juice

Heat oven to 350°F. Spread hazelnuts on ungreased cookie sheet. Bake until golden brown, 4 to 6 minutes, stirring occasionally; cool. Mix with remaining ingredients.

1 SERVING: Calories 245 (Calories from Fat 160); Fat 18g (Saturated 3g); Cholesterol 55mg; Sodium 450mg; Carbohydrate 1g (Dietary Fiber 0g); Protein 20g

Broiled Salmon with Hazelnut Butter

Alfredo Salmon and Noodles

For a flavor of Italy, add 1/3 cup of pesto with sun-dried tomatoes with the remaining ingredients.
If you don't have salmon, use a 6-ounce can of water-packed tuna, drained, instead.

3 cups uncooked wide egg noodles (6 ounces)

1 box (9 ounces) frozen chopped broccoli

1/2 cup Alfredo pasta sauce

1 can (6 ounces) skinless boneless pink salmon,
drained and flaked

1/8 teaspoon pepper

1. Cook noodles as directed on package, adding broccoli for the last 4 to 5 minutes of cooking. Drain and return to saucepan.

2. Stir in remaining ingredients. Cook over low heat 4 to 6 minutes, stirring occasionally, until hot.

1 SERVING: Calories 330 (Calories from Fat 125); Fat 14g (Saturated 7g); Cholesterol 90mg; Sodium 390mg; Carbohydrate 33g (Dietary Fiber 3g); Protein 18g

Alfredo Salmon and Noodles

Marinara Shrimp and Vegetable Bowls

4 SERVINGS

Here's a recipe where "dovetailing," that is, preparing several parts of the recipe at the same time, will save you loads of time. While the water for the pasta comes to a boil, start chopping the veggies. Then, while the pasta cooks, start the shrimp and heat the marinara sauce. Dinner will be ready 1-2-3!

1 package (7 ounces) vermicelli

1 tablespoon olive or vegetable oil

2 cloves garlic, finely chopped

1/2 cup red onion wedges

1 medium zucchini, cut into 2 x 1/4-inch strips

1 medium yellow summer squash, cut into
   2 x 1/4-inch strips

1/4 teaspoon salt

1 pound uncooked, peeled, deveined medium or
   large shrimp, thawed if frozen

1 cup marinara sauce

2 tablespoons chopped fresh or 1/2 teaspoon dried
   basil leaves

1. Cook and drain vermicelli as directed on package. While vermicelli is cooking, heat oil in 10-inch skillet over medium heat. Cook garlic and onion in oil 2 to 3 minutes, stirring frequently, until onion is crisp-tender. Stir in zucchini, yellow squash and salt. Cook 2 to 3 minutes, stirring frequently, just until squash is tender; remove vegetables from skillet.

2. Add shrimp to skillet. Cook and stir 1 to 2 minutes or until shrimp are pink and firm. Meanwhile heat marinara sauce in 1-quart saucepan over medium heat until hot.

3. Divide vermicelli among 4 bowls; toss each serving with about 2 tablespoons marinara sauce. Top with vegetables and shrimp. Drizzle with remaining marinara sauce. Sprinkle with basil.

1 SERVING: Calories 350 (Calories from Fat 65); Fat 7g (Saturated 1g); Cholesterol 105mg; Sodium 580mg; Carbohydrate 56g (Dietary Fiber 4g); Protein 20g

Marinara Shrimp and Vegetable Bowls

Angel Hair Pasta with Shrimp

4 SERVINGS

This is a great meal to make when you want something a bit fancy but don't have a lot of time. Of course, any long pasta will do—fettuccine, spaghetti or angel hair.

1 package (16 ounces) angel hair (capellini) pasta

1/4 cup olive or vegetable oil

2 tablespoons chopped fresh parsley

2 cloves garlic, finely chopped

1 small red chile, seeded and finely chopped

1/3 cup vegetable or chicken broth

1/2 teaspoon freshly grated nutmeg

3/4 pound uncooked, peeled, deveined small shrimp, thawed if frozen

1. Cook and drain pasta as directed on package.

2. While pasta is cooking, heat oil in Dutch oven or 12-inch skillet over medium-high heat. Cook parsley, garlic and chile in oil 1 minute, stirring occasionally. Stir in broth, nutmeg and shrimp; reduce heat. Cover and simmer about 5 minutes or until shrimp are pink and firm.

3. Mix pasta and shrimp mixture in Dutch oven. Cook over medium heat 2 minutes, stirring occasionally.

1 SERVING: Calories 680 (Calories from Fat 160); Fat 17g (Saturated 2.5g); Cholesterol 120mg; Sodium 680mg; Carbohydrate 100g (Dietary Fiber 6g); Protein 32g

Scallop Stir-Fry

4 SERVINGS

The difference between bay scallops and sea scallops is their size. Bay scallops are smaller than sea scallops. If you are using whole bay scallops, you can skip cutting them into smaller pieces.

1 package (3 ounces) Oriental flavor ramen noodles

1 tablespoon olive oil or vegetable oil

3/4 pound asparagus, cut into 1-inch pieces

1 large red bell pepper, cut into thin strips

1 small onion, chopped (1/4 cup)

2 cloves garlic, finely chopped

3/4 pound sea scallops, cut into 1-inch pieces

1 tablespoon soy sauce

2 tablespoons lemon juice

1 teaspoon sesame oil

1/4 teaspoon red pepper sauce

1. Reserve seasoning packet from noodles. Cook and drain noodles as directed on package.

2. While noodles are cooking, heat olive oil in 12-inch skillet over high heat. Add asparagus, bell pepper, onion and garlic; stir-fry 2 to 3 minutes or until vegetables are crisp-tender. Add scallops; stir-fry until white and opaque.

3. Mix contents of reserved seasoning packet, the soy sauce, lemon juice, sesame oil and pepper sauce; stir into scallop mixture. Stir in noodles; heat through.

1 SERVING: Calories 185 (Calories from Fat 65); Fat 7g (Saturated 1g); Cholesterol 25mg; Sodium 580mg; Carbohydrate 12g (Dietary Fiber 2g); Protein 21g

Creamy Crab au Gratin

4 SERVINGS

Fresh mushrooms are available already sliced. When you're in a hurry, what a great time-saver they are! If you happen to have only whole ones around, here's a speedy slicing secret: Use an egg slicer—it works great for mushrooms, too!

2 tablespoons butter or margarine

1 1/2 cups sliced mushrooms (4 ounces)

2 medium stalks celery, sliced (1 cup)

1 can (14 1/2 ounces) chicken broth

3/4 cup half-and-half

3 tablespoons all-purpose flour

1/2 teaspoon red pepper sauce

2 packages (8 ounces each) refrigerated imitation crabmeat chunks or 2 cups chopped cooked crabmeat

1 cup soft bread crumbs (about 1 1/2 slices bread)

1. Heat oven to 400°F. Spray rectangular baking dish, 11 x 7 x 1 1/2 inches, with cooking spray. Melt butter in 10-inch skillet over medium-high heat. Cook mushrooms and celery in butter about 4 minutes, stirring frequently, until celery is tender. Stir in broth. Heat to boiling; reduce heat to medium.

2. Beat half-and-half, flour and pepper sauce with wire whisk until smooth; stir into vegetable mixture. Heat to boiling, stirring constantly. Boil and stir 1 minute. Stir in imitation crabmeat.

3. Spoon imitation crabmeat mixture into baking dish. Top with bread crumbs. Bake uncovered about 15 minutes or until heated through.

1 SERVING: Calories 285 (Calories from Fat 45); Fat 12g (Saturated 6g); Cholesterol 60mg; Sodium 1580mg; Carbohydrate 22g (Dietary Fiber 1g); Protein 23g

Shrimp Pasta Primavera

6 SERVINGS

Want to keep your basil fresh? Instead of refrigerating it, place stems of basil in a glass of water,
and keep on the counter for up to five days.

1 package (10 ounces) rotini pasta

1 cup vegetable or chicken broth

2 cups broccoli flowerets

1/4 pound mushrooms, cut in half

6 ounces feta cheese, crumbled (1 1/2 cups)

1 cup fresh basil leaves, thinly sliced

4 plum (Roma) tomatoes, coarsely chopped

3/4 pound cooked, peeled, deveined large shrimp or
    1 package (12 ounces) frozen, cooked, peeled,
    deveined shrimp, thawed and drained

1. Cook and drain pasta as directed on package.

2. While pasta is cooking, heat broth to boiling in 2-quart saucepan; reduce heat. Stir in broccoli and mushrooms. Cover and simmer about 6 minutes or until broccoli is crisp-tender; remove from heat.

3. Stir in cheese and basil until cheese is melted. Stir in tomatoes and shrimp. Cook uncovered over medium heat, stirring occasionally, just until heated through. Toss with pasta.

1 SERVING: Calories 330 (Calories from Fat 70); Fat 8g (Saturated 5g); Cholesterol 135mg; Sodium 620mg; Carbohydrate 43g (Dietary Fiber 3g); Protein 24g

Shrimp Pasta Primavera

Crab Cakes

6 SERVINGS

How about a different kind of burger tonight? Thaw on-hand buns from the freezer while the crab cakes are cooking and make Crab Cake Sandwiches; top with tartar sauce and serve with oven-baked French fries.

1/4 cup mayonnaise or salad dressing

1 egg

1 1/4 cups soft bread crumbs (about 2 slices bread)

1 teaspoon ground mustard

1/4 teaspoon salt

1/8 teaspoon pepper

2 medium green onions, chopped (2 tablespoons)

2 cans (6 ounces each) crabmeat, drained and flaked*

2 tablespoons vegetable oil

1/4 cup dry bread crumbs

1. Mix mayonnaise and egg in medium bowl. Stir in remaining ingredients except oil and dry bread crumbs. Shape mixture into 6 patties, about 3 inches in diameter.

2. Heat oil in 12-inch skillet over medium heat. Coat each patty with dry bread crumbs. Cook in oil about 10 minutes, turning once, until golden brown and hot in center. Reduce heat if crab cakes brown too quickly.

*Flake crabmeat with a fork and remove any tiny pieces of shell.

1 SERVING: Calories 305 (Calories from Fat 170); Fat 19g (Saturated 3g); Cholesterol 135mg; Sodium 650mg; Carbohydrate 12g (Dietary Fiber 0g); Protein 21g

Crab and Spinach Casserole

4 SERVINGS

As an extra time-saver, use a bag of prewashed spinach for this recipe (tear the larger leaves into 1 1/2-inch pieces). It saves time and eliminates the extra water that would cling to the leaves if you rinsed them yourself.

2 cups uncooked gemelli pasta (4 ounces)

1 package (1.8 ounces) leek soup mix

2 cups milk

1 package (8 ounces) refrigerated imitation crabmeat chunks

2 cups baby spinach leaves, stems removed

1/4 cup freshly shredded Parmesan cheese

1. Heat oven to 350°F. Spray 1 1/2-quart casserole or square baking dish, 8 x 8 x 2 inches, with cooking spray. Cook and drain pasta as directed on package.

2. While pasta is cooking, mix soup mix and milk in 1-quart saucepan. Heat to boiling, stirring constantly. Cut up larger pieces of imitation crabmeat if desired. Mix pasta, crabmeat and spinach in casserole.

3. Pour soup mixture over pasta mixture; stir gently to mix. Spread evenly. Sprinkle with cheese. Bake uncovered about 20 minutes or until bubbly and light golden brown.

1 SERVING: Calories 345 (Calories from Fat 55); Fat 6g (Saturated 2g); Cholesterol 25mg; Sodium 960mg; Carbohydrate 55g (Dietary Fiber 4g); Protein 22g

Crab and Spinach Casserole

Mostly Pasta

Manicotti

7 SERVINGS

This dish offers a great way to get your kids to eat their spinach. Wrapped in cheese and topped in tomato sauce, there's no wonder manicotti is a best-loved recipe by the whole family.

1 jar (32 ounces) chunky-style tomato pasta sauce

2 boxes (9 ounces each) frozen chopped spinach, thawed and well drained

1 container (12 ounces) small-curd creamed cottage cheese (1 1/2 cups)

1 cup grated Parmesan cheese

1 tablespoon snipped fresh or 1 teaspoon dried oregano leaves

1/4 teaspoon pepper

14 uncooked manicotti shells (about 8 ounces)

2 cups shredded mozzarella cheese (8 ounces)

1. Heat oven to 350°F.

2. Spread 1/3 of the pasta sauce in ungreased rectangular baking dish, 13 x 9 x 2 inches. Mix spinach, cottage cheese, Parmesan cheese, oregano and pepper. Fill uncooked manicotti shells with spinach mixture; arrange on pasta sauce in dish.

3. Pour remaining pasta sauce evenly over shells, covering completely; sprinkle with mozzarella cheese. Cover and bake until shells are tender, about 1 1/2 hours.

1 SERVING: Calories 450 (Calories from Fat 145); Fat 16g (Saturated 8g); Cholesterol 35mg; Sodium 1270mg; Carbohydrate 55g (Dietary Fiber 5g); Protein 27g

Vegetable Lasagna

8 SERVINGS

You can also add some shredded carrots, chopped broccoli or sliced mushrooms to this cheesy lasagna to make it even more chock-full of vegetables.

3 cups chunky-style tomato pasta sauce

1 medium zucchini, shredded

6 uncooked lasagna noodles

1 cup ricotta or small-curd creamed cottage cheese

1/4 cup grated Parmesan cheese

1 tablespoon snipped fresh oregano leaves or 1 teaspoon dried oregano leaves

2 cups shredded mozzarella cheese (8 ounces)

1. Heat oven to 350°F.

2. Mix pasta sauce and zucchini. Spread 1 cup mixture in ungreased rectangular baking dish, 11 x 7 x 1 1/2 inches; top with 3 uncooked noodles.

3. Mix ricotta cheese, Parmesan cheese and oregano; spread over noodles in dish. Spread with 1 cup of the sauce mixture.

4. Top with remaining noodles, sauce mixture and the mozzarella cheese. Bake uncovered until hot and bubbly, about 45 minutes. Let stand 15 minutes before cutting.

1 SERVING: Calories 290 (Calories from Fat 110); Fat 12g (Saturated 6g); Cholesterol 25mg; Sodium 700mg; Carbohydrate 32g (Dietary Fiber 2g); Protein 16g

Cheesy Lasagna

12 SERVINGS

It's easy to sing the praises of lasagna—it's cheesy, filling and loved by all ages. And a good lasagna recipe is invaluable when you have to feed a crowd, want a make-ahead meal or need to supply a covered dish.

1/2 cup margarine or butter

1/2 cup all-purpose flour

1/2 teaspoon salt

4 cups milk

1 cup shredded Swiss cheese (4 ounces)

1 cup shredded mozzarella cheese (4 ounces)

1/2 cup grated Parmesan cheese

2 cups small-curd cottage cheese

1/4 cup snipped parsley

1 tablespoon snipped fresh or 1 teaspoon dried
    basil leaves

1/2 teaspoon salt

1 teaspoon snipped fresh or 1/2 teaspoon dried
    oregano leaves

2 cloves garlic, crushed

12 uncooked lasagna noodles

1/2 cup grated Parmesan cheese

1. Heat oven to 350°F.

2. Heat margarine in 2-quart saucepan over low heat until melted. Stir in flour and 1/2 teaspoon salt. Cook, stirring constantly, until smooth and bubbly. Remove from heat; stir in milk. Heat to boiling, stirring constantly. Boil and stir 1 minute.

3. Stir in Swiss cheese, mozzarella cheese and 1/2 cup Parmesan cheese. Cook and stir over low heat until cheeses are melted. Mix remaining ingredients except noodles and remaining Parmesan cheese.

4. Spread 1/4 of the cheese sauce mixture in ungreased rectangular baking dish, 13 x 9 x 2 inches; top with 4 uncooked noodles. Spread 1 cup of the cottage cheese mixture over noodles; spread with 1/4 of the cheese sauce mixture. Repeat with 4 noodles, the remaining cottage cheese mixture, 1/4 of the cheese sauce mixture, the remaining noodles and remaining cheese sauce mixture. Sprinkle with 1/2 cup Parmesan cheese.

5. Bake uncovered until noodles are done, 35 to 40 minutes. Let stand 10 minutes before cutting.

1 SERVING: Calories 325 (Calories from Fat 155); Fat 17g (Saturated 7g); Cholesterol 30mg; Sodium 680mg; Carbohydrate 26g (Dietary Fiber 1g); Protein 18g

Creamy Fettuccine Alfredo

6 SERVINGS

For a creative touch, top with toasted walnuts, roasted red bell pepper strips, or chopped Kalamata olives instead of the parsley.

8 ounces uncooked fettuccine

1/2 cup margarine or butter

1/2 cup whipping (heavy) cream

3/4 cup grated Parmesan cheese

1/2 teaspoon salt

Dash of pepper

Chopped fresh parsley

1. Cook and drain fettuccine as directed on package.

2. While fettuccine is cooking, heat margarine and whipping cream in 2-quart saucepan over low heat, stirring constantly, until margarine is melted. Stir in cheese, salt and pepper.

3. Pour sauce over fettuccine; stir until fettuccine is well coated. Sprinkle with parsley.

1 SERVING: Calories 380 (Calories from Fat 235); Fat 26g (Saturated 9g); Cholesterol 65mg; Sodium 600mg; Carbohydrate 26g (Dietary Fiber 1g); Protein 9g

Countryside Pasta Toss

4 SERVINGS

Frozen baby carrots and sugar snap pea pods can be used if you don't have fresh. Prepare following the package directions before tossing with the other vegetables.

1 cup uncooked rotini pasta (3 ounces)

3/4 pound new potatoes, cut into 1/2-inch wedges

1 cup baby-cut carrots

1 cup broccoli flowerets

1/2 cup sugar snap pea pods

1 tablespoon butter or margarine

2 tablespoons chopped fresh parsley

1 teaspoon dried dill weed

1/2 teaspoon salt

2 ounces fully cooked ham, cut into thin strips

1. Cook and drain pasta as directed on package.

2. While pasta is cooking, place steamer basket in 1/2 inch water in 3-quart saucepan (water should not touch bottom of basket). Place potatoes and carrots in basket. Cover tightly and heat to boiling; reduce heat to medium-low. Steam 5 minutes. Add broccoli and pea pods. Cover and steam about 2 minutes longer or until potatoes are tender.

3. Place vegetables in medium bowl. Add butter, parsley, dill weed and salt; toss. Add ham and pasta; toss.

1 SERVING: Calories 245 (Calories from Fat 45); Fat 5g (Saturated 2g); Cholesterol 15mg; Sodium 550mg; Carbohydrate 45g (Dietary Fiber 5g); Protein 10g

Countryside Pasta Toss

Penne with Vegetables in Tomato-Basil Sauce

4 SERVINGS

2 cups uncooked penne pasta (6 ounces)

1 tablespoon olive or vegetable oil

1 medium onion, chopped (1/2 cup)

1 medium carrot, chopped (1/2 cup)

1 can (14 1/2 ounces) diced tomatoes with basil, garlic and oregano, undrained

1 can (8 ounces) tomato sauce

1 small unpeeled zucchini, chopped (1 cup)

1 tablespoon chopped fresh or 1/2 teaspoon dried basil leaves

2 tablespoons chopped fresh parsley

1/4 cup shredded Parmesan cheese

1. Cook and drain pasta as directed on package.

2. While pasta is cooking, heat oil in 10-inch non-stick skillet over medium-high heat. Cook onion and carrot in oil 2 to 3 minutes, stirring occasionally, until crisp-tender. Stir in tomatoes and tomato sauce. Cook 5 minutes.

3. Stir in zucchini and basil; reduce heat to medium. Cook about 5 minutes, stirring occasionally, until sauce is desired consistency. Stir in parsley. Serve over pasta. Sprinkle with cheese.

1 SERVING: Calories 330 (Calories from Fat 55); Fat 6g (Saturated 2g); Cholesterol 5mg; Sodium 760mg; Carbohydrate 62g (Dietary Fiber 5g); Protein 12g

Penne with Vegetables in Tomato-Basil Sauce

Macaroni and Cheese

6 SERVINGS

Add extra pep to this favorite recipe by using pizza-flavored or jalapeño pepper cheese.

2 cups uncooked elbow macaroni (7 ounces)

1/4 cup margarine or butter

1/4 cup all-purpose flour

1/2 teaspoon salt

1/4 teaspoon pepper

1/4 teaspoon ground mustard

1/4 teaspoon Worcestershire sauce

2 cups milk

2 cups shredded or cubed sharp Cheddar cheese
(8 ounces)

1. Heat oven to 350°F.

2. Cook macaroni as directed on package.

3. While macaroni is cooking, melt margarine in 3-quart saucepan over low heat. Stir in flour, salt, pepper, mustard and Worcestershire sauce. Cook over low heat, stirring constantly, until mixture is smooth and bubbly; remove from heat. Stir in milk. Heat to boiling, stirring constantly. Boil and stir 1 minute. Stir in cheese. Cook, stirring occasionally, until cheese is melted.

4. Drain macaroni. Gently stir macaroni into cheese sauce. Pour into ungreased 2-quart casserole. Bake uncovered 20 to 25 minutes or until bubbly.

1 SERVING: Calories 445 (Calories from Fat 205); Fat 23g (Saturated 11g); Cholesterol 45mg; Sodium 540mg; Carbohydrate 42g (Dietary Fiber 1g); Protein 18g

Pasta with Lemon and Basil

6 SERVINGS

Chop your fresh basil at the last possible moment so the leaves will stay beautiful bright green.

6 ounces angel hair (capellini) pasta

1/4 cup chopped fresh basil leaves

1/4 cup lemon juice

1 tablespoon grated lemon peel

3 tablespoons olive oil

1/2 teaspoon black pepper

Grated Parmesan cheese

1. Cook pasta in boiling water 3 to 5 minutes or just until tender; drain.

2. Toss with remaining ingredients except cheese. Serve with cheese.

1 SERVING: Calories 170 (Calories from Fat 65); Fat 7g (Saturated 1g); Cholesterol 0mg; Sodium 5mg; Carbohydrate 24g (Dietary Fiber 1g); Protein 4g

Pasta with Lemon and Basil

CHAPTER 8

Vegetables & Side Dishes

Roasted Autumn Vegetables

4 SERVINGS

When the crisp, cool evenings of autumn arrive, delight your family with the sweetness of this dish. The slow-roasting of the vegetables helps develop their rich flavor. It makes a perfect partner for roasted chicken.

1/4 cup margarine or butter

1 tablespoon fresh or 1 teaspoon dried sage leaves

1 clove garlic, crushed

1/2 pound Brussels sprouts, cut into halves

1/2 pound parsnips, peeled and cut into 2-inch pieces

1/4 pound baby-cut carrots, peeled

1 small butternut squash, peeled, seeded and cut into 1-inch pieces

1. Heat oven to 375°F.

2. Melt margarine in small saucepan; stir in sage and garlic. Place vegetables in rectangular pan, 13 x 9 x 2 inches. Pour margarine mixture over vegetables; stir to coat.

3. Cover; bake 25 to 30 minutes, stirring occasionally, until vegetables are crisp-tender.

1 SERVING: Calories 170 (Calories from Fat 110); Fat 12g (Saturated 2g); Cholesterol 0mg; Sodium 210mg; Carbohydrate 17g (Dietary Fiber 6g); Protein 5g

Stuffed Zucchini

8 SERVINGS

Summer is the perfect time to use up the pounds of zucchini growing in your garden. This goes well with any chicken recipe.

4 medium zucchini (about 2 pounds)

1 medium onion, chopped (about 1/2 cup)

1/4 cup (1/2 stick) margarine or butter

1 can (4 ounces) chopped green chiles, drained

1 jar (2 ounces) diced pimientos, drained

1 1/2 cups herb-seasoned stuffing mix (dry)

3/4 cup shredded mozzarella or Monterey Jack cheese (3 ounces)

1. Heat 2 inches water (salted if desired) to boiling. Add zucchini. Heat to boiling; reduce heat. Cover and simmer just until tender, 8 to 10 minutes; drain. Cool slightly; cut each zucchini lengthwise in half.

2. Spoon out pulp; chop coarsely. Place zucchini, cut sides up, in ungreased baking dish, 13 x 9 x 2 inches.

3. Heat oven to 350°F.

4. Cook and stir onion in margarine in 10-inch skillet until onion is tender. Stir in chopped pulp, chiles, pimientos and stuffing mix.

5. Divide stuffing mixture among zucchini halves. Sprinkle each with about 1 tablespoon cheese. Bake uncovered until hot, 30 to 35 minutes.

1 SERVING: Calories 145 (Calories from Fat 70); Fat 8g (Saturated 2g); Cholesterol 5mg; Sodium 330mg; Carbohydrate 14g (Dietary Fiber 2g); Protein 6g

Stuffed Zucchini

Warm Caramelized Vegetables

6 SERVINGS

Balsamic vinegar is a great flavor booster, but if you don't have any on hand, you can use cider or red wine vinegar.

2 pounds small red potatoes, cut into 1-inch pieces

1/2 teaspoon salt

1 pound asparagus, cut into 2-inch pieces

1/3 cup butter or margarine

1 large onion, chopped (1 cup)

1/4 cup balsamic vinegar

1/4 cup packed brown sugar

1/4 teaspoon salt

Freshly ground pepper, if desired

1. Heat 1 inch water to boiling in 3-quart saucepan. Add potatoes and 1/2 teaspoon salt. Heat to boiling; reduce heat to medium. Cover and cook about 12 minutes or until tender; drain and set aside.

2. While potatoes are cooking, heat 1 inch water to boiling in 2-quart saucepan. Add asparagus. Heat to boiling; reduce heat to medium. Cover and cook about 5 minutes or until crisp-tender; drain and set aside.

3. While vegetables are cooking, melt butter in 10-inch skillet over medium-high heat. Cook onion in butter about 5 minutes, stirring occasionally, until golden brown. Stir in vinegar, brown sugar and 1/4 teaspoon salt. Pour onion mixture over potatoes and asparagus; stir until coated. Sprinkle with pepper.

1 SERVING: Calories 275 (Calories from Fat 100); Fat 11g (Saturated 6g); Cholesterol 25mg; Sodium 380mg; Carbohydrate 44g (Dietary Fiber 4g); Protein 4g

Warm Caramelized Vegetables

Vegetables with Lemon Butter

12 SERVINGS

The tart lemon butter adds just the right zip to the vegetables. Serve this colorful, tasty side with some broiled fresh fish.

3 bags (10 ounces each) frozen whole green beans

1 1/2 pounds Brussels sprouts, cut into halves

1 pound carrots, peeled and cut into julienne strips

1/2 cup margarine or butter, melted

1 tablespoon grated lemon peel

1 tablespoon lemon juice

1. Cook green beans according to package directions; keep warm.

2. Heat 1 inch water to boiling in large saucepan. Add Brussels sprouts. Cover and heat to boiling; reduce heat. Cook 8 to 10 minutes or until stems are tender; keep warm.

3. Heat 1 inch water to boiling in large saucepan. Add carrots. Cover and heat to boiling; reduce heat. Cook 6 to 8 minutes or until tender; keep warm.

4. Combine margarine, lemon peel and lemon juice. Arrange cooked vegetables on platter; pour margarine mixture over vegetables.

1 SERVING: Calories 110 (Calories from Fat 70); Fat 8g (Saturated 1g); Cholesterol 0mg; Sodium 130mg; Carbohydrate 12g (Dietary Fiber 5g); Protein 3g

Pesto-Stuffed Tomatoes

4 SERVINGS

Speed up this sunny side dish by using one-fourth cup of prepared basil pesto in place of the cheese, nuts, basil, oil, garlic salt and pepper. Just stir the tomato pulp and bread crumbs into the pesto and use to stuff the tomatoes.

4 medium tomatoes (1 1/4 to 1 1/2 pounds)

3 tablespoons shredded Parmesan cheese

2 tablespoons pine nuts

2 tablespoons chopped fresh or 2 teaspoons dried basil leaves

1 1/2 teaspoons olive or vegetable oil

1/2 teaspoon garlic salt

1/4 teaspoon pepper

2 slices bread, torn into crumbs

1. Cut 1/4-inch slice from stem end of each tomato; scoop out pulp. Discard seeds; chop pulp. Mix pulp, 2 tablespoons of the cheese, the nuts, basil, oil, garlic salt and pepper. Gently stir in bread crumbs. Fill tomatoes with mixture.

2. Place each tomato in 6-ounce custard cup, or arrange tomatoes in circle in shallow round microwavable dish. Cover loosely with waxed paper.

3. Microwave on High 3 to 4 minutes or until tender. Sprinkle with remaining 1 tablespoon cheese. Cover and let stand about 2 minutes or until cheese is melted.

1 SERVING: Calories 120 (Calories from Fat 55); Fat 6g (Saturated 2g); Cholesterol 5mg; Sodium 290mg; Carbohydrate 13g (Dietary Fiber 2g); Protein 5g

Pesto-Stuffed Tomatoes

Caesar Vegetable Medley

6 SERVINGS

Tired of the same old vegetables? Add a flavor boost with Caesar dressing mix in place of ordinary seasoning.

2 tablespoons olive or vegetable oil

2 bags (1 pound each) frozen cauliflower, carrots and snow pea pods (or other combination)

1 envelope (1.2 ounces) Caesar dressing mix

1. Heat oil in 10-inch nonstick skillet over medium-high heat.

2. Cover and cook frozen vegetables and dressing mix (dry) in oil 5 to 7 minutes, stirring frequently, until vegetables are crisp-tender.

1 SERVING: Calories 85 (Calories from Fat 45); Fat 5g (Saturated 1g); Cholesterol 0mg; Sodium 380mg; Carbohydrate 13g (Dietary Fiber 6g); Protein 3g

Baked Corn on the Cob with Herbs

4 SERVINGS

For a tantalizing blend of flavors, team two herbs together with the corn—basil and rosemary, or thyme and dill weed are especially good combinations. Serve with plenty of melted butter to drizzle over the top.

4 ears fresh corn

Cooking spray

1/4 teaspoon salt

1/8 teaspoon pepper

20 to 24 sprigs fresh basil, rosemary, thyme, dill weed, marjoram or sage

1. Heat oven to 450°F. Husk and remove silk from corn. Place each ear on 12-inch square of aluminum foil. Spray on all sides with cooking spray. Sprinkle with salt and pepper. Place 5 to 6 sprigs of fresh herbs around each ear. Seal foil.

2. Place sealed ears of corn directly on oven rack. Bake about 20 minutes or until corn is tender.

1 SERVING: Calories 110 (Calories from Fat 10); Fat 1g (Saturated 0g); Cholesterol 0mg; Sodium 610mg; Carbohydrate 25g (Dietary Fiber 3g); Protein 3g

Baked Corn on the Cob with Herbs

Cheesy Broccoli-Rice Bake

8 SERVINGS

2 tablespoons butter or margarine

1 large onion, chopped (1 cup)

1 loaf (16 ounces) prepared cheese product,
   cut into cubes

1 can (10 3/4 ounces) condensed cream of
   mushroom soup

2/3 cup milk

1/4 teaspoon pepper, if desired

2 cups 1/2-inch pieces broccoli flowerets

3 cups cooked rice

1 cup fine soft bread crumbs (about
   1 1/2 slices bread)

2 tablespoons butter or margarine, melted

1. Heat oven to 350°F. Grease rectangular baking
   dish, 13 x 9 x 2 .

2. Melt 2 tablespoons butter in 10-inch skillet over
   medium-high heat. Cook onion in butter, stirring occasionally, until crisp-tender; reduce heat
   to medium. Stir in cheese, soup, milk and pepper.
   Cook, stirring frequently, until cheese is melted.

3. Stir in broccoli and rice. Spoon into baking dish.
   Mix bread crumbs and 2 tablespoons melted butter; sprinkle over rice mixture. Bake uncovered
   30 to 35 minutes or until light brown on top and
   bubbly around edges.

1 SERVING: Calories 445 (Calories from Fat 245); Fat 27g
(Saturated 16g); Cholesterol 70mg; Sodium 1250mg;
Carbohydrate 34g (Dietary Fiber 2g); Protein 18g

Rice Pilaf

4 SERVINGS

2 tablespoons butter or margarine

1 small onion, chopped (1/4 cup)

1 cup uncooked regular long-grain rice

2 cups chicken broth

1/4 teaspoon salt

1. Melt butter in 3-quart saucepan over medium
   heat. Cook onion in butter about 3 minutes,
   stirring occasionally, until tender.

2. Stir in rice. Cook 5 minutes, stirring frequently.
   Stir in broth and salt.

3. Heat to boiling, stirring once or twice; reduce
   heat to low. Cover and simmer 16 minutes (do
   not lift cover or stir); remove from heat. Let stand
   covered 5 minutes.

1 SERVING (ABOUT 3/4 CUP): Calories 245 (Calories from
Fat 65); Fat 7g (Saturated 4g); Cholesterol 15mg; Sodium
1250mg; Carbohydrate 41g (Dietary Fiber 1g); Protein 6g

Curry Pilaf: Stir in 1/2 cup diced dried fruit and
raisin mixture, 1/4 teaspoon ground allspice, 1/4 teaspoon ground turmeric and 1/4 teaspoon curry
powder with the broth and salt in step 2.

Mushroom Pilaf: Stir in 1 can (4 ounces) mushroom pieces and stems, drained, with the broth and
salt in step 2.

Mushroom, Tomato and Basil Orzo Pilaf

1 1/3 cups uncooked orzo (rosamarina) pasta
   (8 ounces)

1/4 cup pine nuts

2 teaspoons olive or vegetable oil

1 clove garlic, finely chopped

1 cup sliced mushrooms (3 ounces)

4 medium green onions, sliced (1/4 cup)

1 cup sliced plum (Roma) tomatoes

2 tablespoons chopped fresh or 2 teaspoons dried
   basil leaves

1/4 teaspoon salt

1 teaspoon olive or vegetable oil

1. Cook and drain pasta as directed on package.
   While pasta is cooking, cook nuts in 12-inch skillet over medium heat 2 to 3 minutes, stirring
   constantly, until toasted. Remove from skillet.

2. Add 2 teaspoons oil and the garlic to skillet.
   Cook and stir over medium-high heat 1 minute.
   Stir in mushrooms and onions. Cook about
   2 minutes, stirring occasionally, until onions are
   crisp-tender.

3. Stir in tomatoes, pasta, basil, salt and remaining
   teaspoon oil. Cook over medium heat, stirring
   occasionally, until heated through. Spoon into
   serving dish; sprinkle with nuts.

1 SERVING (ABOUT 3/4 CUP): Calories 135 (Calories from
Fat 25); Fat 3g (Saturated 1g); Cholesterol 0mg; Sodium 80mg;
Carbohydrate 25g (Dietary Fiber 2g); Protein 6g

Au Gratin Potatoes

2 tablespoons butter or stick margarine

1 small onion, chopped (1/4 cup)

1 tablespoon all-purpose flour

1/2 teaspoon salt

1/4 teaspoon pepper

2 cups milk

2 cups shredded natural sharp Cheddar cheese
   (8 ounces)

6 medium potatoes, peeled and thinly sliced (6 cups)

1/4 cup dry bread crumbs

Paprika, if desired

1. Heat oven to 375°F.

2. Melt butter in 2-quart saucepan over medium
   heat. Cook onion in butter about 2 minutes,
   stirring occasionally, until tender. Stir in flour,
   salt and pepper. Cook, stirring constantly, until
   bubbly; remove from heat.

3. Stir in milk. Heat to boiling, stirring constantly.
   Boil and stir 1 minute; remove from heat. Stir in
   1 1/2 cups of the cheese until melted.

4. Spread potatoes in ungreased 1 1/2-quart casserole.
   Pour cheese sauce over potatoes. Bake uncovered
   1 hour.

5. Mix remaining 1/2 cup cheese and the bread
   crumbs; sprinkle over potatoes. Sprinkle with
   paprika. Bake uncovered 15 to 20 minutes or until
   top is brown and bubbly and potatoes are tender.

1 SERVING: Calories 340 (Calories from Fat 160); Fat 18g
(Saturated 11g); Cholesterol 55mg; Sodium 540mg;
Carbohydrate 31g (Dietary Fiber 2g); Protein 15g

Roasted Rosemary-Onion Potatoes

4 SERVINGS

Roasted potatoes, redolent with rosemary and sweet onion, is a great side dish.

4 medium potatoes (1 1/3 pounds)

1 small onion, finely chopped (1/4 cup)

2 tablespoons olive or vegetable oil

**2 tablespoons chopped fresh or 2 teaspoons dried
rosemary leaves**

**1 teaspoon chopped fresh or 1/4 teaspoon dried
thyme leaves**

1/4 teaspoon salt

1/8 teaspoon pepper

1. Heat oven to 450°F. Grease jelly roll pan,
   15 1/2 x 10 1/2 x 1 inch.

2. Cut potatoes into 1-inch chunks. Mix onion, oil,
   rosemary, thyme, salt and pepper in large bowl.
   Add potatoes; toss to coat. Spread potatoes in
   single layer in pan.

3. Bake uncovered 20 to 25 minutes, turning occasionally, until potatoes are light brown and tender
   when pierced with fork.

1 SERVING: Calories 150 (Calories from Fat 65); Fat 7g
(Saturated 1g); Cholesterol 0mg; Sodium 140mg; Carbohydrate
22g (Dietary Fiber 2g); Protein 2g

Roasted Rosemary-Onion Potatoes

Garlic Smashed Potatoes

6 medium Yukon Gold or russet potatoes (2 pounds)

1 bulb garlic

2 tablespoons olive or vegetable oil

1 teaspoon chopped fresh or 1/4 teaspoon dried oregano leaves

1/2 teaspoon salt

1/3 to 1/2 cup milk

1/4 cup chopped fresh chives

1. Heat oven to 375°F. Pierce potatoes with fork to allow steam to escape. Cut 1/4-inch slice from top of garlic bulb to expose cloves. Carefully remove most of the paperlike skin, leaving the bulb intact and the cloves unpeeled. Wrap garlic in aluminum foil. Bake potatoes and garlic about 1 hour or until potatoes are tender.

2. Heat oil and oregano over medium heat 2 to 3 minutes or until oregano is fragrant.

3. Open garlic pack to cool. Cut potatoes in half; carefully spoon potatoes in large bowl. Save skins for another use or discard. Separate garlic cloves and press the cloves slightly to squeeze the garlic out; discard skin. Place garlic in bowl; add oil mixture and salt.

4. Mash potatoes until no lumps remain. Beat in milk in small amounts (amount of milk needed to make potatoes smooth and fluffy depends on kind of potatoes). Beat vigorously until potatoes are light and fluffy. Stir in chives.

1 SERVING: Calories 155 (Calories from Fat 45); Fat 5g (Saturated 1g); Cholesterol 2mg; Sodium 190mg; Carbohydrate 26g (Dietary Fiber 2g); Protein 3g

Duchess Potatoes

Think of this side dish the next time you are having a roast. And if company is coming, they can be made ahead of time. Just pop them in the oven before serving.

12 medium potatoes (4 pounds), peeled

2/3 to 1 cup milk

1/2 cup margarine, butter or spread, softened

1/2 teaspoon salt

Dash of pepper

4 eggs, beaten

Margarine, butter or spread, melted

1. Cut potatoes into large pieces if desired. Heat 1 inch water (salted if desired) to boiling in Dutch oven. Add potatoes. Cover and heat to boiling; reduce heat. Cook whole potatoes 30 to 35 minutes, pieces 20 to 25 minutes, or until tender; drain. Shake pan gently over low heat to dry potatoes.

2. Heat oven to 425°F. Grease cookie sheet.

3. Mash potatoes until no lumps remain. Beat in milk in small amounts (amount of milk needed to make potatoes smooth and fluffy depends on kind of potatoes). Add 1/2 cup margarine, the salt and pepper. Beat vigorously until potatoes are light and fluffy. Add eggs; beat until blended.

4. Drop potato mixture by 12 spoonfuls into mounds on cookie sheet. Or place in decorating bag with star tip and form rosettes or pipe a border around meat or fish. Brush with melted margarine. Bake about 15 minutes or until light brown.

1 SERVING: Calories 240 (Calories from Fat 115); Fat 13g (Saturated 3g); Cholesterol 70mg; Sodium 260mg; Carbohydrate 28g (Dietary Fiber 2g); Protein 5g

Twice-Baked Potatoes

8 SERVINGS

These potatoes can be put in the fridge or freezer (wrapped up tightly) before being baked again. Bake refrigerated potatoes 30 minutes; frozen potatoes about 40 minutes.

4 large baking potatoes (8 to 10 ounces each)

1/4 to 1/2 cup milk

1/4 cup margarine or butter, softened

1/4 teaspoon salt

Dash of pepper

1 cup shredded Cheddar cheese (4 ounces)

1 tablespoon chopped fresh chives

1. Heat oven to 375°F. Gently scrub potatoes, but do not peel. Pierce potatoes several times with fork to allow steam to escape while potatoes bake.

2. Bake 1 hour to 1 hour 15 minutes or until potatoes feel tender when pierced in center with fork.

3. When potatoes are cool enough to handle, cut lengthwise in half; scoop out inside, leaving a thin shell. Mash potatoes in medium bowl with potato masher or electric mixer on low speed until no lumps remain. Add milk in small amounts, beating after each addition with potato masher or electric mixer on low speed (amount of milk needed to make potatoes smooth and fluffy depends on kind of potatoes used).

4. Add butter, salt and pepper; beat vigorously until potatoes are light and fluffy. Stir in cheese and chives. Fill potato shells with mashed potato mixture. Place on ungreased cookie sheet.

5. Increase oven temperature to 400°F. Bake about 20 minutes or until hot.

1 SERVING: Calories 180 (Calories from Fat 100); Fat 11g (Saturated 7g); Cholesterol 30mg; Sodium 210mg; Carbohydrate 16g (Dietary Fiber 1g); Protein 5g

CHAPTER 9

Desserts

Angel Food Cake with Chocolate Glaze

16 SERVINGS

If you're looking for a delicious dessert that has done the skinny on fat and cholesterol, look no further. Angel food cake boasts zero to both! Serve it with cut-up fresh fruit or berries and a dollop of fluffy whipped topping and it will be a favorite with both young and old.

1 1/2 cups powdered sugar

1 cup cake flour

1 1/2 cups egg whites (about 12)

1 1/2 teaspoons cream of tartar

1 cup granulated sugar

1 1/2 teaspoons vanilla

1/2 teaspoon almond extract

1/4 teaspoon salt

Chocolate Glaze (right)

1. Move oven rack to lowest position. Heat oven to 375°F.

2. Mix powdered sugar and flour; set aside. Beat egg whites and cream of tartar in large bowl with electric mixer on medium speed until foamy. Beat in granulated sugar, 2 tablespoons at a time, on high speed, adding vanilla, almond extract and salt with the last addition of sugar. Continue beating until stiff and glossy meringue forms. Do not underbeat.

3. Sprinkle sugar-flour mixture, 1/4 cup at a time, over meringue, folding in just until sugar-flour mixture disappears. Push batter into ungreased angel food cake pan (tube pan), 10 x 4 inches. Cut gently through batter with metal spatula.

4. Bake 30 to 35 minutes or until cracks feel dry and top springs back when touched lightly. Immediately turn pan upside down onto heatproof funnel or bottle. Let stand about 2 hours or until cake is completely cool. Loosen side of cake with knife or long, metal spatula; remove from pan.

5. Spread or drizzle top of cake with Chocolate Glaze.

CHOCOLATE GLAZE

1/2 cup semisweet chocolate chips

2 tablespoons margarine or butter

2 tablespoons corn syrup

1 to 2 teaspoons hot water

Heat chocolate chips, margarine and corn syrup in 1-quart saucepan over low heat, stirring constantly, until chocolate chips are melted; cool slightly. Stir in hot water, 1 teaspoon at a time, until consistency of thick syrup.

1 SERVING: Calories 180 (Calories from Fat 25); Fat 3g (Saturated 1g); Cholesterol 0mg; Sodium 95mg; Carbohydrate 35g (Dietary Fiber 0g); Protein 3g

Best Chocolate Cake with Fudge Frosting

Looking for a great cake to make for someone's birthday? Here it is! For a special color and flavor treat, serve a few raspberries with each slice!

2 cups all-purpose flour

2 cups sugar

1/2 cup shortening

3/4 cup water

3/4 cup buttermilk

1 teaspoon baking soda

1 teaspoon salt

1 teaspoon vanilla

1/2 teaspoon baking powder

2 eggs

4 ounces unsweetened chocolate, melted
    and cooled

Fudge Frosting (right)

1. Heat oven to 350°F. Grease and flour rectangular pan, 13 x 9 x 2 inches, 3 round pans, 8 x 1 1/2 inches, or 2 round pans, 9 x 1 1/2 inches. Beat all ingredients except Fudge Frosting in large bowl on low speed 30 seconds, scraping bowl constantly. Beat on high speed 3 minutes, scraping bowl occasionally. Pour into pans.

2. Bake rectangular pan 40 to 45 minutes, round pans 30 to 35 minutes or until toothpick inserted in center comes out clean. Cool rounds 10 minutes; remove from pans. Cool completely. Prepare Fudge Frosting; frost cake. Fill layers with 1/3 cup frosting; frost side and top with remaining frosting.

FUDGE FROSTING

2 cups sugar

1/2 cup shortening

3 ounces unsweetened chocolate

2/3 cup milk

1/2 teaspoon salt

2 teaspoons vanilla

Mix all ingredients except vanilla in 2 1/2-quart saucepan. Heat to rolling boil, stirring occasionally. Boil 1 minute without stirring. Place saucepan in bowl of ice and water. Beat until frosting is smooth and of spreading consistency; stir in vanilla.

1 SERVING: Calories 620 (Calories from Fat 250); Fat 28g (Saturated 10g); Cholesterol 40mg; Sodium 450mg; Carbohydrate 89g (Dietary Fiber 3g); Protein 6g

Best Chocolate Cake with Fudge Frosting

Chocolate Swirl Cake

16 SERVINGS

Check your chocolate—baking chocolate works best in this recipe. Melted chocolate chips will harden when dropped onto the batter, making it difficult to swirl.

3 cups Original Bisquick mix

3/4 cup sugar

1/4 cup shortening

1 cup cold milk or water

1 tablespoon vanilla

2 eggs

2 ounces semisweet baking chocolate, melted and cooled

Chocolate Frosting (right)

1. Heat oven to 350°F. Grease and flour rectangular pan, 13 x 9 x 2 inches. Beat all ingredients except chocolate and Chocolate Frosting in large bowl with electric mixer on low speed 30 seconds, scraping bowl constantly. Beat on medium speed 4 minutes, scraping bowl occasionally.

2. Pour 3 cups of the batter into pan. Beat melted chocolate into remaining batter on medium speed until well blended. Drop chocolate batter randomly by tablespoonfuls onto white batter. Swirl knife through batters for swirled design.

3. Bake 30 to 35 minutes or until toothpick inserted in center comes out clean. Cool completely, about 1 hour. Frost with Chocolate Frosting.

CHOCOLATE FROSTING

1/3 cup margarine or butter, softened

2 ounces unsweetened baking chocolate, melted and cooled

2 cups powdered sugar

1 1/2 teaspoons vanilla

About 2 tablespoons milk

Stir margarine and chocolate in medium bowl until blended. Stir in remaining ingredients. Beat until smooth and spreadable.

1 SERVING: Calories 300 (Calories from Fat 115); Fat 13g (Saturated 4g); Cholesterol 25mg; Sodium 380mg; Carbohydrate 43g (Dietary Fiber 1g); Protein 3g

Fudge Pudding Cake

9 SERVINGS

They'll think it's magic! A fudgy chocolate pudding cake that "bakes" right in the microwave. Let it cook while you have dinner—then add ice cream or whipped topping and enjoy it nice and warm for dessert.

1 cup all-purpose flour

3/4 cup granulated sugar

2 tablespoons baking cocoa

2 teaspoons baking powder

1/4 teaspoon salt

1/2 cup milk

2 tablespoons vegetable oil

1 teaspoon vanilla

1 cup chopped nuts

1 cup packed brown sugar

1/4 cup baking cocoa

1 3/4 cups boiling water

1. Mix flour, granulated sugar, 2 tablespoons cocoa, the baking powder and salt in 2-quart microwavable casserole.

2. Stir in milk, oil and vanilla. Stir in nuts. Spread evenly in casserole. Mix brown sugar and 1/4 cup cocoa; sprinkle over batter. Pour boiling water over batter.

3. Microwave uncovered on Medium (50%) 9 minutes; rotate casserole 1/2 turn. Microwave uncovered on High 5 to 6 minutes or until top is almost dry. Serve warm with ice cream or whipped cream.

1 SERVING: Calories 345 (Calories from Fat 180); Fat 13g (Saturated 2g); Cholesterol 0mg; Sodium 140mg; Carbohydrate 56g (Dietary Fiber 3g); Protein 4g

Fudge Pudding Cake

Applesauce Cake

16 SERVINGS

The applesauce in this one-bowl cake makes for a moist and delicious cake. Want a really yummy idea?
Serve this cake with warmed caramel topping drizzled over each slice. Pure heaven!

2 1/2 cups all-purpose flour

1 1/2 cups unsweetened applesauce

1 1/4 cups sugar

1/2 cup margarine or butter, softened

1/2 cup water

1 1/2 teaspoons baking soda

1 1/2 teaspoons pumpkin pie spice

1 teaspoon salt

3/4 teaspoon baking powder

2 eggs

1 cup raisins

2/3 cup chopped nuts

Maple-Nut Buttercream Frosting or Cream Cheese Frosting (right), if desired

1. Heat oven to 350°F. Grease bottom and sides of rectangular pan, 13 x 9 x 2 inches, or 2 round pans, 8 x 1 1/2 or 9 x 1 1/2 inches, with shortening; lightly flour.

2. Beat all ingredients except raisins, nuts and Maple-Nut Buttercream Frosting in large bowl with electric mixer on low speed 30 seconds, scraping bowl constantly. Beat on high speed 3 minutes, scraping bowl occasionally. Stir in raisins and nuts. Pour into pan(s).

3. Bake rectangle 45 to 50 minutes, rounds 40 to 45 minutes, or until toothpick inserted in center comes out clean. Cool rectangle in pan on wire rack. Cool rounds 10 minutes; remove from pans to wire rack. Cool completely.

4. Frost rectangle or fill and frost layers with Maple-Nut Buttercream Frosting. If you use Cream Cheese Frosting, cover and store frosted cake in the refrigerator.

MAPLE-NUT BUTTERCREAM FROSTING

3 cups powdered sugar

1/3 cup margarine or butter, softened

1/2 cup maple-flavored syrup

1 to 2 tablespoons milk

1/4 cup finely chopped nuts

Mix powdered sugar and margarine in medium bowl. Stir in syrup and milk. Beat until smooth and spreadable. Stir in nuts.

CREAM CHEESE FROSTING

1 package (8 ounces) cream cheese, softened

1/4 cup margarine or butter, softened

2 teaspoons milk

1 teaspoon vanilla

4 cups powdered sugar

Beat cream cheese, margarine, milk and vanilla in medium bowl with electric mixer on low speed until smooth. Gradually beat in powdered sugar on low speed, 1 cup at a time, until smooth and spreadable.

1 SERVING: Calories 265 (Calories from Fat 90); Fat 10g (Saturated 2g); Cholesterol 25mg; Sodium 350mg; Carbohydrate 42g (Dietary Fiber 1g); Protein 3g

Carrot Cake

1 1/2 cups sugar

1 cup vegetable oil

3 large eggs

2 cups all-purpose flour*

2 teaspoons ground cinnamon

1 teaspoon baking soda

1 teaspoon vanilla

1/2 teaspoon salt

3 cups shredded carrots (5 medium)

1 cup coarsely chopped nuts

Cream Cheese Frosting (page 154), if desired

1. Heat oven to 350°F. Grease bottom and sides of rectangular pan, 13 x 9 x 2 inches, or 2 round pans, 8 x 1 1/2 or 9 x 1 1/2 inches, with shortening; lightly flour.

2. Beat sugar, oil and eggs in large bowl with electric mixer on low speed about 30 seconds or until blended. Add remaining ingredients except carrots, nuts and Cream Cheese Frosting; beat on low speed 1 minute. Stir in carrots and nuts. Pour into pan(s).

3. Bake rectangle 40 to 45 minutes, rounds 30 to 35 minutes, or until toothpick inserted in center comes out clean. Cool rectangle in pan on wire rack. Cool rounds 10 minutes; remove from pans to wire rack. Cool completely, about 1 hour.

4. Frost rectangle or fill round layers and frost with Cream Cheese Frosting. Store covered in refrigerator.

*If using self-rising flour, omit baking soda and salt.

1 SERVING: Calories 430 (Calories from Fat 235); Fat 26g (Saturated 4g); Cholesterol 55mg; Sodium 230mg; Carbohydrate 46g (Dietary Fiber 2g); Protein 5g

Apple Cake: Substitute 3 cups chopped tart apples (3 medium) for the carrots.

Pineapple-Carrot Cake: Add 1 can (8 ounces) crushed pineapple, drained, and 1/2 cup flaked or shredded coconut with the carrots.

Zucchini Cake: Substitute 3 cups shredded zucchini for the carrots.

Carrot Cake

Oatmeal Spice Cake with Browned Butter Frosting

16 SERVINGS

Sugar and spice and all things nice make this a cake to remember! Top with vanilla ice cream for a little à la mode. Keep an eye on the butter when you make the frosting. You'll have more control over the browning if you use a heavy skillet and just let the frosting get light golden brown to ensure it won't burn.

1 1/2 cups all-purpose flour

1 cup quick-cooking oats

1 cup packed brown sugar

1/2 cup granulated sugar

1 1/2 teaspoons baking soda

1 teaspoon ground cinnamon

1/2 teaspoon salt

1/2 teaspoon ground nutmeg, if desired

1/2 cup shortening

1 cup water

2 eggs

2 tablespoons molasses

Browned Butter Frosting (above right)

1. Heat oven to 350°F.

2. Grease rectangular pan, 13 x 9 x 2 inches with shortening; lightly flour.

3. Beat all ingredients except Browned Butter Frosting with electric mixer in large bowl 30 seconds on low speed, scraping bowl constantly. Beat on high speed 3 minutes, scraping bowl occasionally. Pour into pan.

4. Bake 35 to 40 minutes or until toothpick inserted in center comes out clean. Cool in pan on wire rack. Prepare Browned Butter Frosting; spread on cake.

BROWNED BUTTER FROSTING

1/3 cup butter

3 cups powdered sugar

1 1/2 teaspoons vanilla

About 2 tablespoons milk

Heat butter over medium heat until delicate brown. Mix in powdered sugar. Beat in vanilla and enough milk until smooth and spreadable.

1 SERVING: Calories 330 (Calories from Fat 100); Fat 11g (Saturated 4g); Cholesterol 35mg; Sodium 230mg; Carbohydrate 56g (Dietary Fiber 1g); Protein 3g

Caramel-Apple Cake

6 SERVINGS

For a festive presentation, sprinkle the dish with ground cinnamon or nutmeg.

1 1/2 cups Original Bisquick mix

2/3 cup granulated sugar

1/2 cup milk

**2 medium cooking apples, peeled and
    sliced (2 cups)**

1 tablespoon lemon juice

3/4 cup packed brown sugar

1/2 teaspoon ground cinnamon

1 cup boiling water

Ice cream or whipped cream, if desired

1. Heat oven to 350°F. Mix Bisquick and granulated sugar in medium bowl. Stir in milk until blended.

2. Pour batter into ungreased square pan, 9 x 9 x 2 inches. Top with apples; sprinkle with lemon juice. Mix brown sugar and cinnamon; sprinkle over apples. Pour boiling water over apples.

3. Bake 50 to 60 minutes or until toothpick inserted in center comes out clean. Serve warm with ice cream.

1 SERVING: Calories 355 (Calories from Fat 45); Fat 5g (Saturated 1g); Cholesterol 0mg; Sodium 450mg; Carbohydrate 75g (Dietary Fiber 1g); Protein 3g

Williamsburg Orange Cake

It's not hard to make your own buttermilk. Try mixing 1 1/2 tablespoons of vinegar or lemon juice into regular milk and waiting a few minutes for it to thicken.

2 1/2 cups all-purpose flour or 2 3/4 cups cake flour

1 1/2 cups sugar

1 1/2 teaspoons baking soda

3/4 teaspoon salt

1 1/2 cups buttermilk

1/2 cup margarine or butter, softened

1/4 cup shortening

3 eggs

1 1/2 teaspoons vanilla

1 cup golden raisins, cut up

1/2 cup finely chopped nuts

1 tablespoon grated orange peel

Williamsburg Butter Frosting (above right)

1. Heat oven to 350°F. Grease and flour rectangular pan, 13 x 9 x 2 inches. Beat all ingredients except frosting in large mixer bowl on low speed, scraping bowl constantly, 30 seconds. Beat on high speed, scraping bowl occasionally, 3 minutes. Pour into pans.

2. Bake until toothpick inserted in center comes out clean, 45 to 50 minutes; cool. Frost with Williamsburg Butter Frosting.

WILLIAMSBURG BUTTER FROSTING

1/2 cup margarine or butter, softened

4 1/2 cups powdered sugar

4 to 5 tablespoons orange-flavored liqueur or orange juice

1 tablespoon grated orange peel

Mix margarine and powdered sugar. Beat in liqueur and orange peel.

1 SERVING: Calories 500 (Calories from Fat 170); Fat 19g (Saturated 4g); Cholesterol 40mg; Sodium 420mg; Carbohydrate 78g (Dietary Fiber 1g); Protein 5g

Lemon Chiffon Cake

12 SERVINGS

2 cups all-purpose flour * or 2 1/4 cups cake flour

1 1/2 cups sugar

3 teaspoons baking powder

1 teaspoon salt

3/4 cup cold water

1/2 cup vegetable oil

2 teaspoons vanilla

1 tablespoon grated lemon peel

7 large egg yolks (with all-purpose flour) or 5 large egg yolks (with cake flour)

1 cup large egg whites (about 8)

1/2 teaspoon cream of tartar

Vanilla Glaze, if desired (right)

1. Move oven rack to lowest position. Heat oven to 325°F. Mix flour, sugar, baking powder and salt in large bowl. Beat in water, oil, vanilla, lemon peel and egg yolks with electric mixer on low speed until smooth.

2. With clean beaters, beat egg whites and cream of tartar in large bowl with electric mixer on high speed until stiff peaks form. Gradually pour egg yolk mixture over beaten egg whites, folding in with rubber spatula just until blended. Pour into ungreased angel food cake pan (tube pan), 10 x 4 inches.

3. Bake about 1 hour 15 minutes or until top springs back when touched lightly. Immediately turn pan upside down onto heatproof funnel or bottle. Let hang about 2 hours or until cake is completely cool. Loosen side of cake with knife or long metal spatula; remove from pan.

4. Spread Vanilla or Lemon Glaze over top of cake, allowing some to drizzle down side.

*If using self-rising flour, omit baking powder and salt.

1 SERVING: Calories 295 (Calories from Fat 108); Fat 12g (Saturated 2g); Cholesterol 125mg; Sodium 360mg; Carbohydrate 42g (Dietary Fiber 1g); Protein 6g

VANILLA GLAZE

1/3 cup butter or margarine*

2 cups powdered sugar

1 1/2 teaspoons vanilla or clear vanilla

2 to 4 tablespoons hot water

Melt butter in 1 1/2-quart saucepan over low heat; remove from heat. Stir in powdered sugar and vanilla. Stir in hot water, 1 tablespoon at a time, until smooth and consistency of thick syrup.

*Do not use vegetable oil spreads.

Lemon Glaze: Stir 1/2 teaspoon grated lemon peel into melted butter. Substitute lemon juice for the vanilla and hot water.

Pineapple Upside-Down Cake

8 SERVINGS

1/4 cup margarine or butter

1/4 cup packed brown sugar

1 can (8 ounces) sliced pineapple, drained and cut in half

2 tablespoons chopped pecans, if desired

Maraschino cherries, if desired

1 1/2 cups Original Bisquick mix

1/2 cup granulated sugar

1/2 cup milk or water

2 tablespoons vegetable oil

1 teaspoon vanilla

1 egg

1. Heat oven to 350°F. Melt margarine in round pan, 9 x 1 1/4 inches, or square pan, 8 x 8 x 2 inches, in oven. Sprinkle brown sugar over margarine. Arrange pineapple slices in single layer on sugar mixture. Sprinkle with pecans. Place cherry in center of each pineapple slice (cherries with stems can be added after baking).

2. Beat remaining ingredients in large bowl with electric mixer on low speed 30 seconds, scraping bowl constantly. Beat on medium speed 4 minutes, scraping bowl occasionally. Pour batter over pineapple.

3. Bake 30 to 35 minutes or until toothpick inserted in center comes out clean. Immediately turn pan upside down onto heatproof serving plate; leave pan over cake a few minutes. Remove pan. Let cake stand at least 10 minutes before serving.

1 SERVING: Calories 305 (Calories from Fat 135); Fat 15g (Saturated 3g); Cholesterol 25mg; Sodium 410mg; Carbohydrate 42g (Dietary Fiber 2g); Protein 3g

Banana Upside-Down Cake: Omit pineapple, cherries and pecans. Sprinkle 2 tablespoons chopped walnuts over brown sugar mixture in pan. Cut 2 bananas into slices; arrange on brown sugar mixture.

Pear Upside-Down Cake: Substitute 1 large pear, thinly sliced, for the pineapple.

Raspberry Upside-Down Cake: Substitute 1 1/2 cups raspberries for the pineapple, granulated sugar for the brown sugar and sliced almonds for the pecans. Omit cherries. Decrease vanilla to 1/2 teaspoon; add 1/2 teaspoon almond extract.

Pineapple Upside-Down Cake

Cream Cheese Pound Cake

10 SERVINGS

If you have cake left over, you can make a Cream Cheese Trifle: Cut the cake into large cubes, and place them in a large glass or plastic bowl. Sprinkle with a little orange juice, cover with plastic wrap and refrigerate about 2 hours. Layer cake, whipped cream and fresh fruit in goblets. Cover and refrigerate at least 1 hour before serving.

3 cups Original Bisquick mix

1 1/2 cups granulated sugar

3/4 cup margarine or butter, softened

1/2 cup all-purpose flour

1 teaspoon vanilla

1/8 teaspoon salt

6 eggs

1 package (8 ounces) cream cheese, softened

Powdered sugar, if desired

1. Heat oven to 350°F. Grease and flour 12-cup bundt cake pan or 2 loaf pans, 9 x 5 x 3 inches.

2. Beat all ingredients except powdered sugar in large bowl with electric mixer on low speed 30 seconds, scraping bowl frequently. Beat on medium speed 4 minutes, scraping bowl occasionally. Pour into pan.

3. Bake 55 to 60 minutes or until toothpick inserted near center comes out clean. Cool 5 minutes. Turn pan upside down onto wire rack or heatproof serving plate; remove pan. Cool cake completely, about 1 hour. Sprinkle with powdered sugar.

1 SERVING: Calories 535 (Calories from Fat 270); Fat 30g (Saturated 10g); Cholesterol 150mg; Sodium 830mg; Carbohydrate 58g (Dietary Fiber 1g); Protein 9g

Cream Cheese Pound Cake

Strawberry Shortcakes

6 SERVINGS

Who can resist tender shortcakes covered in sweet strawberries and topped off with a bit of whipped cream!
Blueberries, raspberries, fresh peaches, kiwi and cherries also make wonderful fruits for these shortcakes.

1 quart strawberries, sliced

1/2 cup sugar

1/3 cup shortening

2 cups all-purpose flour

2 tablespoons sugar

3 teaspoons baking powder

1 teaspoon salt

3/4 cup milk

Margarine or butter, softened

Sweetened whipped cream

1. Mix strawberries and 1/2 cup sugar. Let stand 1 hour.

2. Heat oven to 450°F.

3. Cut shortening into flour, 2 tablespoons sugar, the baking powder and salt in medium bowl, using pastry blender or crisscrossing 2 knives, until mixture looks like fine crumbs. Stir in milk just until blended.

4. Turn dough onto lightly floured surface. Gently smooth into a ball. Knead 20 to 25 times. Roll 1/2 inch thick. Cut into 3-inch squares or use floured 3-inch cutter. Place about 1 inch apart on ungreased cookie sheet.

5. Bake 10 to 12 minutes or until golden brown.

6. Split shortcakes horizontally in half while hot. Spread margarine on split sides. Fill with strawberries; replace tops. Top with strawberries and sweetened whipped cream.

1 SERVING: Calories 400 (Calories from Fat 135); Fat 15g (Saturated 5g); Cholesterol 10mg; Sodium 630mg; Carbohydrate 63g (Dietary Fiber 8g); Protein 6g

Strawberry Shortcakes

Cheesecake with Cherry Glaze

16 SERVINGS

We're sure you'll receive rave reviews for this "never fail" cheesecake! You might want to use a 15-ounce can of cherry, or blueberry, pie filling instead of making the Cherry Glaze.

1/2 cup fine zwieback or graham cracker crumbs

1 tablespoon sugar

1/4 teaspoon ground cinnamon

1/4 teaspoon ground nutmeg

5 eggs, separated

1 cup sugar

2 packages (8 ounces each) cream cheese, softened

1 cup sour cream

2 tablespoons all-purpose flour

1 teaspoon vanilla

Cherry Glaze (right)

1. Heat oven to 275°F. Butter springform pan, 9 x 3 inches.

2. Mix cracker crumbs, 1 tablespoon sugar, the cinnamon and nutmeg. Dust bottom and side of springform pan with crumb mixture.

3. Beat egg yolks in large bowl with electric mixer on high speed or until thick and lemon-colored. Gradually beat in 1 cup sugar. Beat in cream cheese until smooth. Beat in sour cream, flour and vanilla until smooth.

4. Beat egg whites in large bowl with electric mixer on high speed until stiff but not dry. Gently fold into cream cheese mixture. Pour into pan.

5. Bake 1 hour 10 minutes. Turn off oven and leave cheesecake in oven 1 hour. Cool in pan on wire rack 15 minutes. Refrigerate about 3 hours or until chilled.

6. Spread top of cheesecake with Cherry Glaze. Refrigerate until glaze is set. Remove cheesecake from pan just before serving.

CHERRY GLAZE

1 can (16 ounces) pitted red tart cherries, drained and liquid reserved

1/2 cup sugar

2 tablespoons cornstarch

Few drops red food color, if desired

Add enough water to cherry liquid to measure 1 cup. Mix sugar and cornstarch in 1 1/2-quart saucepan. Gradually stir in cherry liquid. Cook over medium heat, stirring constantly, until mixture thickens and boils. Boil and stir 1 minute; remove from heat. Stir in cherries and food color; cool.

1 SERVING: Calories 275 (Calories from Fat 135); Fat 15g (Saturated 9g); Cholesterol 105mg; Sodium 115mg; Carbohydrate 30g (Dietary Fiber 0g); Protein 5g

Turtle Cheesecake

12 SERVINGS

**1 1/2 cups finely crushed vanilla wafer cookies
(about 40 cookies)**

1/4 cup butter or margarine, melted*

2 packages (8 ounces each) cream cheese, softened

1/2 cup sugar

2 teaspoons vanilla

2 eggs

1/4 cup hot fudge topping

1 cup caramel topping

1/2 cup coarsely chopped pecans

1. Heat oven to 350°F. Mix cookie crumbs and butter in medium bowl. Press firmly against bottom and side of pie plate, 9 x 1 1/4 inches.

2. Beat cream cheese, sugar, vanilla and eggs in large bowl with electric mixer on low speed until smooth. Pour half of the mixture into pie plate.

3. Add hot fudge topping to remaining cream cheese mixture in bowl; beat on low speed until smooth. Spoon over vanilla mixture in pie plate. Swirl mixtures slightly with tip of knife.

4. Bake 40 to 50 minutes or until center is set. (Do not insert knife into cheesecake because the hole may cause cheesecake to crack as it cools.) Cool at room temperature 1 hour. Refrigerate at least 2 hours until chilled. Serve with caramel topping and pecans. Store covered in refrigerator.

*Spreads with at least 65% vegetable oil can be used.

1 SERVING: Calories 440 (Calories from Fat 235); Fat 26g (Saturated 13g); Cholesterol 90mg; Sodium 340mg; Carbohydrate 46g (Dietary Fiber 1g); Protein 6g

Turtle Cheesecake

Pumpkin Cheesecake

12 SERVINGS

Try this tempting alternative to the traditional Thanksgiving pumpkin pie. The gingersnap crust adds a nice spice to the moist, rich cheesecake. Dot with whipped cream and garnish with pecan halves around the edges of the cake for a festive look.

1 1/4 cups gingersnap cookie crumbs (about twenty 2-inch cookies)

1/4 cup margarine or butter, melted

3 packages (8 ounces each) cream cheese, softened

1 cup sugar

1 teaspoon ground cinnamon

1 teaspoon ground ginger

1/2 teaspoon ground cloves

1 can (16 ounces) pumpkin

4 eggs

2 tablespoons sugar

12 walnut halves

3/4 cup chilled whipping cream

1. Heat oven to 350°F.

2. Mix cookie crumbs and margarine. Press evenly on bottom of springform pan, 9 x 3 inches. Bake 10 minutes; cool.

3. Reduce oven temperature to 300°F.

4. Beat cream cheese, 1 cup sugar, the cinnamon, ginger and cloves in 4-quart bowl on medium speed until smooth and fluffy. Add pumpkin. Beat in eggs, one at a time, on low speed. Pour over crumb mixture.

5. Bake until center is firm, about 1 1/4 hours. Cool to room temperature. Cover and refrigerate at least 3 hours but no longer than 48 hours.

6. Cook and stir 2 tablespoons sugar and the walnuts over medium heat until sugar is melted and nuts are coated. Immediately spread on a dinner plate or aluminum foil; cool. Carefully break nuts apart to separate if necessary. Cover tightly and store at room temperature up to 3 days.

7. Loosen cheesecake from side of pan; remove side of pan. Beat whipping cream in chilled 1 1/2-quart bowl until stiff. Pipe whipped cream around edge of cheesecake; arrange walnuts on top. Refrigerate any remaining cheesecake immediately.

1 SERVING: Calories 450 (Calories from Fat 290); Fat 32g (Saturated 17g); Cholesterol 150mg; Sodium 310mg; Carbohydrate 33g (Dietary Fiber 1g); Protein 8g

Pumpkin Cheesecake

Fresh Peach Cobbler

6 SERVINGS

If you're short on time, try using blueberries instead—there's no peeling or pitting to do!

1/2 cup sugar

1 tablespoon cornstarch

1/4 teaspoon ground cinnamon

4 cups sliced peaches (6 medium)

1 teaspoon lemon juice

3 tablespoons shortening

1 cup all-purpose flour

1 tablespoon sugar

1 1/2 teaspoons baking powder

1/2 teaspoon salt

1/2 cup milk

Sweetened whipped cream, if desired

1. Heat oven to 400°F. Mix 1/2 cup sugar, the cornstarch and cinnamon in 2-quart saucepan. Stir in peaches and lemon juice. Cook, stirring constantly, until mixture thickens and boils. Boil and stir 1 minute. Pour into ungreased 2-quart casserole; keep peach mixture hot in oven.

2. Cut shortening into flour, 1 tablespoon sugar, the baking powder and salt in medium bowl, using pastry blender or crisscrossing 2 knives, until mixture looks like fine crumbs. Stir in milk. Drop dough by 6 spoonfuls onto hot peach mixture.

3. Bake 25 to 30 minutes or until topping is golden brown. Serve warm with sweetened whipped cream.

1 SERVING: Calories 260 (Calories from Fat 65); Fat 7g (Saturated 2g); Cholesterol 5mg; Sodium 310mg; Carbohydrate 48g (Dietary Fiber 2g); Protein 3g

Kiwi-Berry Tarts

6 SERVINGS

If you don't have apple jelly on hand, you can use raspberry jelly or seedless raspberry jam instead.

1 cup Original Bisquick mix

2 tablespoons sugar

1 tablespoon margarine or butter, softened

2 packages (3 ounces each) cream cheese, softened

1/4 cup sugar

1/4 cup sour cream

1 1/2 cups assorted berries (raspberries, strawberries, blueberries)

2 kiwifruit, peeled and sliced

1/3 cup apple jelly, melted

1. Heat oven to 375°F. Mix Bisquick, 2 tablespoons sugar, the margarine and 1 package cream cheese in small bowl until dough forms a ball.

2. Divide dough into 6 parts. Press dough on bottom and 3/4 inch up side of 6 tart pans, 4 1/4 x 1 inch, or 10-ounce custard cups. Place on cookie sheet. Bake 10 to 12 minutes or until light brown; cool on wire rack. Remove tart shells from pans.

3. Beat remaining package of cream cheese, 1/4 cup sugar and the sour cream with electric mixer on medium speed until smooth. Spoon into tart shells, spreading over bottoms. Top with berries and kiwifruit. Brush with jelly. Store covered in refrigerator.

1 SERVING: Calories 335 (Calories from Fat 155); Fat 17g (Saturated 8g); Cholesterol 35mg; Sodium 410mg; Carbohydrate 44g (Dietary Fiber 3g); Protein 4g

Kiwi-Berry Tarts

Impossibly Easy French Apple Pie

8 SERVINGS

Streusel Topping (right)

3 large all-purpose apples (Braeburn, Gala or Haralson), peeled and thinly sliced (3 cups)

1/2 cup Original Bisquick mix

1/2 cup sugar

1/2 cup milk

1 tablespoon margarine or butter, softened

1 teaspoon ground cinnamon

1/4 teaspoon ground nutmeg

2 eggs

1. Heat oven to 350°F. Grease pie plate, 9 x 1 1/4 inches. Make Streusel Topping; set aside. Spread apples in pie plate.

2. In separate bowl, stir remaining ingredients until blended. Pour over apples. Sprinkle with topping.

3. Bake 40 to 45 minutes or until knife inserted in center comes out clean. Cool 5 minutes.

STREUSEL TOPPING

1/2 cup Original Bisquick mix

1/4 cup chopped nuts

1/4 cup packed brown sugar

2 tablespoons firm margarine or butter

Mix Bisquick, nuts and brown sugar. Cut in margarine, using fork or pastry blender, until mixture is crumbly.

1 SERVING: Calories 235 (Calories from Fat 90); Fat 10g (Saturated 2g); Cholesterol 55mg; Sodium 290mg; Carbohydrate 33g (Dietary Fiber 1g); Protein 4g

Impossibly Easy Peach Pie: Substitute 2 cans (16 ounces each) sliced peaches, well drained, or 4 medium peaches, peeled and sliced (3 cups), for the apples.

Impossibly Easy French Apple Pie

Lemon Meringue Pie

8 SERVINGS

Carefully measure the water and lemon juice in the filling. That way you'll get the right consistency to hold a cut.

Baked Pie Crust (page 175)

3 egg yolks

1 1/2 cups sugar

1/3 cup plus 1 tablespoon cornstarch

1 1/2 cups water

3 tablespoons margarine or butter

2 teaspoons grated lemon peel

1/2 cup lemon juice

2 drops yellow food color, if desired

Meringue (right)

1. Prepare Baked Pie Crust. Heat oven to 350°F.

2. Beat egg yolks with fork in small bowl. Mix sugar and cornstarch in 2-quart saucepan. Gradually stir in water. Cook over medium heat, stirring constantly, until mixture thickens and boils. Boil and stir 1 minute.

3. Immediately stir at least half of the hot mixture into egg yolks; stir back into hot mixture in saucepan. Boil and stir 2 minutes.* Stir in margarine, lemon peel, lemon juice and food color. Press plastic wrap on filling to prevent a tough layer from forming on top.

4. Prepare Meringue. Pour hot lemon filling into pie crust. Spoon onto hot pie filling. Spread over filling, carefully sealing meringue to edge of crust to prevent shrinking or weeping.

5. Bake about 15 minutes or until meringue is light brown. Cool away from draft 2 hours. Cover and refrigerate cooled pie until serving.** Immediately refrigerate any remaining pie.

MERINGUE

3 egg whites

1/4 teaspoon cream of tartar

6 tablespoons sugar

1/2 teaspoon vanilla

Beat egg whites and cream of tartar in medium bowl with electric mixer on high speed until foamy. Beat in sugar, 1 tablespoon at a time; continue beating until stiff and glossy. Do not underbeat. Beat in vanilla.

*Do not boil less than 2 minutes or filling may stay too soft or become runny.

**This pie is best served the day it is made. If refrigerated more than 1 day, the filling may become soft.

1 SERVING: Calories 425 (Calories from Fat 145); Fat 16g (Saturated 4g); Cholesterol 80mg; Sodium 210mg; Carbohydrate 66g (Dietary Fiber 0g); Protein 4g

Lemon Meringue Pie

Strawberry Glacé Pie

When backyard gardens and farmer's markets flourish with summer fruits, use other seasonal fruits in this pie.
Try 6 cups of raspberries or 5 cups of sliced fresh peaches for the strawberries.

Baked Pie Crust (below)

1 1/2 quarts strawberries

1 cup sugar

3 tablespoons cornstarch

1/2 cup water

1 package (3 ounces) cream cheese, softened

1. Prepare Baked Pie Crust.

2. Mash enough strawberries to measure 1 cup. Mix sugar and cornstarch in 2-quart saucepan. Gradually stir in water and mashed strawberries. Cook over medium heat, stirring constantly, until mixture thickens and boils. Boil and stir 1 minute; cool.

3. Beat cream cheese until smooth. Spread in pie shell. Fill shell with whole strawberries. Pour cooked strawberry mixture over top. Refrigerate about 3 hours or until set. Refrigerate any remaining pie after serving.

BAKED PIE CRUST

1/3 cup plus 1 tablespoon shortening or 1/3 cup lard

1 cup all-purpose flour

1/4 teaspoon salt

2 to 3 tablespoons cold water

1. Heat oven to 475°F.

2. Cut shortening into flour and salt, using pastry blender or crisscrossing 2 knives, until particles are size of coarse crumbs. Sprinkle with cold water, 1 tablespoon at a time, tossing with fork until all flour is moistened and pastry almost cleans side of bowl (1 to 2 teaspoons water can be added if necessary). Gather pastry into a ball.

3. Shape into flattened round on lightly floured cloth-covered board. Roll pastry into circle 2 inches larger than upside-down pie plate, 9 x 1 1/4 inches, with floured cloth-covered rolling pin. Fold pastry into fourths; place in pie plate.

4. Unfold and ease into plate, pressing firmly against bottom and side. Trim overhanging edge of pastry 1 inch from rim of plate. Fold and roll pastry under, even with plate; flute.

5. Prick bottom and side thoroughly with fork. Bake 8 to 10 minutes or until light brown; cool on wire rack.

1 SERVING: Calories 315 (Calories from Fat 125); Fat 14g (Saturated 5g); Cholesterol 10mg; Sodium 180mg; Carbohydrate 47g (Dietary Fiber 3g); Protein 3g

Cherry-Berries on a Cloud

10 TO 12 SERVINGS

Lots of requests come in for this recipe and we know why! You, too, will be on cloud nine after one bite of this sweet very-berry pie. The juicy cherries and fresh fruit sit on a cloud of marshmallow and whipped cream, making this dessert irresistibly good.

Pastry Crust (right)

1 package (8 ounces) cream cheese, softened

3/4 cup sugar

1 teaspoon vanilla

2 cups whipping (heavy) cream

2 1/2 cups miniature marshmallows

1 can (21 ounces) cherry pie filling

1 teaspoon lemon juice

2 cups sliced strawberries (1 pint) or 1 bag
   (16 ounces) frozen strawberries, thawed

1 cup fresh or frozen (thawed) sliced peaches

1. Prepare and bake Pastry Crust.

2. Beat cream cheese, sugar and vanilla in large bowl with electric mixer on medium speed until smooth. Beat whipping cream in chilled medium bowl with electric mixer on high speed until stiff. Fold whipped cream and marshmallows into cream cheese mixture; spread over crust.

3. Cover and refrigerate at least 8 hours but no longer than 48 hours.

4. Mix pie filling, lemon juice, strawberries and peaches. Cut dessert into serving pieces; serve with fruit mixture. Cover and refrigerate any remaining dessert.

PASTRY CRUST

1 1/2 cups all-purpose flour

1 cup margarine or butter, softened

1/2 cup powdered sugar

Heat oven to 400°F. Beat all ingredients with electric mixer on low speed 1 minute, scraping bowl constantly. Beat on medium speed about 2 minutes or until creamy. Spread in ungreased rectangular pan, 13 x 9 x 2 inches. Bake 12 to 15 minutes or until edges are golden brown. Cool completely. (For quick cooling, place in freezer 10 to 15 minutes.)

1 SERVING: Calories 650 (Calories from Fat 370); Fat 41g (Saturated 19g); Cholesterol 80mg; Sodium 310mg; Carbohydrate 67g (Dietary Fiber 2g); Protein 5g

Cherry-Berries on a Cloud

Fluffy Key Lime Pie

8 SERVINGS

A native Florida fruit, Key limes are smaller, rounder, more yellow in color and more tart than the prevalent green Persian limes. If Key limes aren't available in your grocery store, look for bottled Key lime juice near the other bottled lime juices.

Pat-in-the-Pan Pie Crust (right)

1 can (14 ounces) sweetened condensed milk (not evaporated)

1/2 cup Key lime juice or regular lime juice

1 container (8 ounces) frozen whipped topping, thawed

1 tablespoon grated lime peel

Lime slices, if desired

1. Make Pat-in-the-Pan Pie Crust.

2. Beat condensed milk and lime juice in large bowl with electric mixer on medium speed until smooth and thickened. Fold in whipped topping and lime peel. Spoon into pie crust.

3. Cover and refrigerate about 2 hours or until set. Garnish with lime slices. Store covered in refrigerator.

PAT-IN-THE-PAN PIE CRUST

1 cup Original Bisquick mix

1/4 cup margarine or butter, softened

2 tablespoons boiling water

Heat oven to 400°F. Mix Bisquick and margarine in medium bowl. Add boiling water; stir vigorously until very soft dough forms. Press dough firmly in pie plate, 9 x 1 1/4 inches, bringing dough onto rim of plate, using fingers dusted with Bisquick mix. Flute edge if desired. Freeze 15 minutes. Bake 8 to 10 minutes or until light golden brown. Cool completely on wire rack, about 30 minutes.

1 SERVING: Calories 355 (Calories from Fat 135); Fat 15g (Saturated 8g); Cholesterol 40mg; Sodium 340mg; Carbohydrate 48g (Dietary Fiber 0g); Protein 7g

Fluffy Key Lime Pie

Chocolate Brownies

16 BROWNIES

You can make colorful Thanksgiving turkeys, festive holiday wreaths or delicate Valentine hearts, but any day you bake up these tender brownies becomes a holiday.

2/3 cup margarine or butter

5 ounces unsweetened baking chocolate, cut into pieces

1 3/4 cups sugar

2 teaspoons vanilla

3 eggs

1 cup all-purpose flour

1 cup chopped walnuts

Fudge Frosting (page 151), if desired

1. Heat oven to 350°F. Grease bottom and sides of square pan, 9 x 9 x 2 inches, with shortening.

2. Melt margarine and chocolate in 1-quart saucepan over low heat, stirring constantly. Cool slightly.

3. Beat sugar, vanilla and eggs in medium bowl with electric mixer on high speed 5 minutes. Beat in chocolate mixture on low speed. Beat in flour just until blended. Stir in walnuts. Spread in pan.

4. Bake 40 to 45 minutes or just until brownies begin to pull away from sides of pan. Cool completely in pan on wire rack. Spread with Fudge Frosting. Cut into about 2-inch squares.

1 BROWNIE: Calories 300 (Calories from Fat 160); Fat 18g (Saturated 5g); Cholesterol 40mg; Sodium 100mg; Carbohydrate 32g (Dietary Fiber 2g); Protein 4g

Lemon Squares

25 SQUARES

You'll love these tart and creamy lemon bars. Be sure to grate the lemon peel first. Then firmly roll the lemon on your countertop before squeezing to get the most juice you can from the lemon.

1 cup all-purpose flour

1/2 cup margarine or butter, softened

1/4 cup powdered sugar

1 cup granulated sugar

2 teaspoons grated lemon peel, if desired

2 tablespoons lemon juice

1/2 teaspoon baking powder

1/4 teaspoon salt

2 eggs

1. Heat oven to 350°F.

2. Mix flour, margarine and powdered sugar. Press in ungreased square pan, 8 x 8 x 2 or 9 x 9 x 2 inches, building up 1/2-inch edges.

3. Bake crust 20 minutes.

4. Beat remaining ingredients with electric mixer on high speed about 3 minutes or until light and fluffy. Pour over hot crust.

5. Bake 25 to 30 minutes or until no indentation remains when touched lightly in center. Cool in pan on wire rack. Cut into about 1 1/2-inch squares.

1 SQUARE: Calories 90 (Calories from Fat 35); Fat 4g (Saturated 1g); Cholesterol 15mg; Sodium 80mg; Carbohydrate 13g (Dietary Fiber 0g); Protein 1g

Snickerdoodles

ABOUT 6 DOZEN COOKIES

They are as fun to say as they are to eat. This can be a great way to get the kids involved in helping to roll the dough in the cinnamon-sugar mixture. Or, for a colorful twist, roll the dough in colored sugar instead of white granulated sugar.

1 1/2 cups sugar

1/2 cup margarine or butter, softened

1/2 cup shortening

2 eggs

2 3/4 cups all-purpose flour

2 teaspoons cream of tartar

1 teaspoon baking soda

1/4 teaspoon salt

2 tablespoons sugar

2 teaspoons ground cinnamon

1. Heat oven to 400°F.

2. Mix 1 1/2 cups sugar, the margarine, shortening and eggs thoroughly in 3-quart bowl. Stir in flour, cream of tartar, baking soda and salt until blended. Shape dough by rounded teaspoonfuls into balls.

3. Mix 2 tablespoons sugar and the cinnamon; roll balls in sugar mixture. Place about 2 inches apart on ungreased cookie sheet. Bake until set, 8 to 10 minutes. Immediately remove from cookie sheet.

1 COOKIE: Calories 65 (Calories from Fat 25); Fat 3g (Saturated 1g); Cholesterol 5mg; Sodium 45mg; Carbohydrate 8g (Dietary Fiber 0g); Protein 1g

Oatmeal-Raisin Cookies

ABOUT 3 DOZEN COOKIES

Looking for something to replace the raisins? Try dried cherries or dried cranberries for a refreshing change of flavor and color.

2/3 cup granulated sugar

2/3 cup packed brown sugar

1/2 cup margarine or butter, softened

1/2 cup shortening

1 teaspoon baking soda

1 teaspoon ground cinnamon

1 teaspoon vanilla

1/2 teaspoon baking powder

1/2 teaspoon salt

2 eggs

3 cups quick-cooking or old-fashioned oats

1 cup all-purpose flour

1 cup raisins, chopped nuts or semisweet chocolate chips, if desired

1. Heat oven to 375°F.

2. Mix all ingredients except oats, flour and raisins in large bowl. Stir in oats, flour and raisins.

3. Drop dough by rounded tablespoonfuls about 2 inches apart onto ungreased cookie sheet.

4. Bake 9 to 11 minutes or until light brown. Immediately remove from cookie sheet. Cool on wire rack.

1 COOKIE: Calories 120 (Calories from Fat 55); Fat 6g (Saturated 1g); Cholesterol 10mg; Sodium 110mg; Carbohydrate 15g (Dietary Fiber 1g); Protein 2g

Chocolate Chip Cookies

ABOUT 4 1/2 DOZEN COOKIES

For perfectly shaped cookies, use a small ice-cream scoop to drop cookie dough onto the cookie sheet.

1/2 cup margarine or butter, softened

1 cup packed brown sugar

2 teaspoons vanilla

1 egg

2 3/4 cups Original Bisquick mix

1 bag (6 ounces) semisweet chocolate chips (1 cup)

1/2 cup chopped nuts, if desired

1. Heat oven to 375°F. Mix margarine, brown sugar, vanilla and egg in large bowl. Stir in Bisquick mix, chocolate chips and nuts.

2. Drop dough by rounded teaspoonfuls about 2 inches apart onto ungreased cookie sheet; flatten slightly.

3. Bake about 10 minutes or until golden brown. Remove from cookie sheet to wire rack.

1 COOKIE: Calories 80 (Calories from Fat 35); Fat 4g (Saturated 1g); Cholesterol 5mg; Sodium 115mg; Carbohydrate 10g (Dietary Fiber 0g); Protein 1g

Caramel Turtle Bars

24 BARS

Think outside the square! For triangle shapes, cut squares diagonally in half. For diamond shapes, first cut parallel lines 1 or 1 1/2 inches apart down the length of the pan, then cut diagonal lines 1 or 1 1/2 inches apart across the straight cuts.

1 1/2 cups Original Bisquick mix

1 cup quick-cooking oats

3/4 cup packed brown sugar

1/3 cup margarine or butter, softened

1 egg

1 bag (14 ounces) caramels, unwrapped

2 tablespoons milk

1 cup chopped pecans

3/4 cup semisweet chocolate chips

1. Heat oven to 350°F. Stir Bisquick mix, oats, brown sugar, margarine and egg until well blended. Press in bottom of ungreased rectangular pan, 13 x 9 x 2 inches. Bake about 15 minutes or until golden brown; cool.

2. Heat caramels and milk in 2-quart saucepan over low heat, stirring frequently, until caramels are melted. Spread over crust. Sprinkle pecans evenly over caramels. Heat chocolate chips over low heat, stirring frequently, until melted. Drizzle over pecans.

3. Cool 30 minutes. For bars, cut into 6 rows by 4 rows.

1 BAR: Calories 220 (Calories from Fat 90); Fat 10g (Saturated 3g); Cholesterol 10mg; Sodium 190mg; Carbohydrate 31g (Dietary Fiber 1g); Protein 3g

Caramel Turtle Bars and Chocolate Chip Cookies

Helpful Nutrition Information

Nutrition Guidelines

We provide nutrition information for each recipe that includes calories, fat, cholesterol, sodium, carbohydrate, fiber and protein. Individual food choices can be based on this information.

Recommended intake for a daily diet of 2,000 calories as set by the Food and Drug Administration

Total Fat . . . . .Less than 65g

Saturated Fat . . . . .Less than 20g

Cholesterol . . . . .Less than 300mg

Sodium .Less than 2,400mg

Total Carbohydrate 300g

Dietary Fiber 25g

Criteria Used for Calculating Nutrition Information

- The first ingredient was used wherever a choice is given (such as 1/3 cup sour cream or plain yogurt).

- The first ingredient amount was used wherever a range is given (such as 3- to 3-1/2–pound cut-up broiler-fryer chicken).

- The first serving number was used wherever a range is given (such as 4 to 6 servings).

- "If desired" ingredients and recipe variations were not included (such as sprinkle with brown sugar, if desired).

- Only the amount of a marinade or frying oil that is estimated to be absorbed by the food during preparation or cooking was calculated.

Ingredients Used in Recipe Testing and Nutrition Calculations

- Ingredients used for testing represent those that the majority of consumers use in their homes: large eggs, 2% milk, 80%-lean ground beef, canned ready-to-use chicken broth and vegetable oil spread containing not less than 65 percent fat.

- Fat-free, low-fat or low-sodium products were not used, unless otherwise indicated.

- Solid vegetable shortening (not butter, margarine, nonstick cooking sprays or vegetable oil spread as they can cause sticking problems) was used to grease pans, unless otherwise indicated.

Equipment Used in Recipe Testing

We use equipment for testing that the majority of consumers use in their homes. If a specific piece of equipment (such as a wire whisk) is necessary for recipe success, it is listed in the recipe.

- Cookware and bakeware without nonstick coatings were used, unless otherwise indicated.

- No dark-colored, black or insulated bakeware was used.

- When a pan is specified in a recipe, a metal pan was used; a baking dish or pie plate means ovenproof glass was used.

- An electric hand mixer was used for mixing only when mixer speeds are specified in the recipe directions. When a mixer speed is not given, a spoon or fork was used.

Index

Page numbers in *italics* indicate illustrations.